Student Affairs and the Law

Margaret J. Barr, *Editor*

NEW DIRECTIONS FOR STUDENT SERVICES

URSULA DELWORTH and GARY R. HANSON, *Editors-in-Chief*

Number 22, June 1983

Paperback sourcebooks in
The Jossey-Bass Higher Education Series

Jossey-Bass Inc., Publishers
San Francisco • Washington • London

Margaret J. Barr (Ed.).
Student Affairs and the Law.
New Directions for Student Services, no. 22.
San Francisco: Jossey-Bass, 1983.

New Directions for Student Services Series
Ursula Delworth and Gary R. Hanson, *Editors-in-Chief*

New Directions for Student Services (publication number USPS
449-070) is published quarterly by Jossey-Bass Inc., Publishers.
Second-class postage rates paid at San Francisco, California,
and at additional mailing offices.

Correspondence:
Subscriptions, single-issue orders, change of address notices,
undelivered copies, and other correspondence should be sent to
New Directions Subscriptions, Jossey-Bass Inc., Publishers,
433 California Street, San Francisco, California 94104.

Editorial correspondence should be sent to the Editors-in-Chief,
Ursula Delworth, University Counseling Service, Iowa
Memorial Union, University of Iowa, Iowa City, Iowa 52242
or Gary R. Hanson, Office of the Dean of Students,
Student Services Building, Room 101, University of Texas
at Austin, Austin, Texas 78712.

Library of Congress Catalogue Card Number LC 82-84204
International Standard Serial Number ISSN 0164-7970
International Standard Book Number ISBN 87589-970-6

Cover art by Willi Baum
Manufactured in the United States of America

Ordering Information

The paperback sourcebooks listed below are published quarterly and can be ordered either by subscription or single-copy.

Subscriptions cost $35.00 per year for institutions, agencies, and libraries. Individuals can subscribe at the special rate of $21.00 per year *if payment is by personal check.* (Note that the full rate of $35.00 applies if payment is by institutional check, even if the subscription is designated for an individual.) Standing orders are accepted. Subscriptions normally begin with the first of the four sourcebooks in the current publication year of the series. When ordering, please indicate if you prefer your subscription to begin with the first issue of the *coming* year.

Single copies are available at $7.95 when payment accompanies order, and *all single-copy orders under $25.00 must include payment.* (California, New Jersey, New York, and Washington, D.C., residents please include appropriate sales tax.) For billed orders, cost per copy is $7.95 plus postage and handling. (Prices subject to change without notice.)

Bulk orders (ten or more copies) of any individual sourcebook are available at the following discounted prices: 10–49 copies, $7.15 each; 50–100 copies, $6.35 each; over 100 copies, *inquire.* Sales tax and postage and handling charges apply as for single copy orders.

To ensure correct and prompt delivery, all orders must give either the *name of an individual* or an *official purchase order number.* Please submit your order as follows:

Subscriptions: specify series and year subscription is to begin.
Single Copies: specify sourcebook code (such as, SS8) and first two words of title.

Mail orders for United States and Possessions, Latin America, Canada, Japan, Australia, and New Zealand to:
Jossey-Bass Inc., Publishers
433 California Street
San Francisco, California 94104

Mail orders for all other parts of the world to:
Jossey-Bass Limited
28 Banner Street
London EC1Y 8QE

New Directions for Student Services Series
Ursula Delworth and Gary R. Hanson, *Editors-in-Chief*

SS1 *Evaluating Program Effectiveness,* Gary R. Hanson
SS2 *Training Competent Staff,* Ursula Delworth
SS3 *Reducing the Dropout Rate,* Lee Noel
SS4 *Applying New Developmental Findings,* Lee Knefelkamp, Carole Widick, Clyde A. Parker

Contents

Editor's Notes

We all would agree that the work world of a dean of men or a dean of women thirty years ago is very different from the work world of a vice-president of student affairs or a dean of students today. Behavioral mores have changed, student populations have altered, and society's expectations of higher education have expanded. As part of these changes, the unilateral power and authority of college administrators have also diminished. Through court cases, statutes, and other legal channels, the legal rights of members of the university community are being vigorously enforced. Thus, higher education reflects society at large, which increasingly uses the courts to settle differences. For the student affairs administrator, legal constraints and legal challenges can profoundly affect service delivery and programs.

Unfortunately, most student affairs administrators do not have a strong background in the law. A good understanding of the law and current issues under litigation can be very useful. This volume is not intended to be a definitive work on the relationship of student affairs to legal issues. Instead, it has been designed to bridge the knowledge gap by highlighting some pressing issues of concern.

Chapter One acquaints the student affairs professional with the many sources of legal constraints on university actions. In Chapter Two, Frank Ardaiolo provides a comprehensive overview of due process requirements for students in cases of alleged academic or behavioral misconduct. His chapter provides concrete suggestions to help us all as we review our policies and procedures in this sensitive area.

In recent years, a number of court cases have been successfully litigated on the basis of a breach of contract between the student and the institution. In Chapter Three, George Shur provides a comprehensive overview of this emerging body of law and raises some pertinent questions. University facilities are often sought for use by nonaffiliated groups and individuals. In Chapter Four, I provide some guidance on the development of policies for facilities use that administrators can use in day-by-day operations. In Chapter Five, a student affairs administrator and two attorneys who practice in a campus setting discuss the relationship of the university to student organizations. Finally, Shari Rhode provides guidance to the uninitiated on the proper role of university legal counsel and how we can avoid problems through cooperation.

This sourcebook includes a list of sources of additional assistance and a glossary of legal terms. Finally, all cases cited in the text appear in a list of cases. The notations after the case title indicate which court heard the case.

Cases cited in this volume are listed in full in Appendix 2.

1

Citations with "U.S.," "S.Ct." are Supreme Court cases. The note *F. 2d* indicates the case was heard at the federal circuit level and the parentheses at the end of the citation indicate which circuit heard the case. The citation *F. Supp.* indicates that the case was heard at a federal district court. Any case with a citation like *A. 2d, Mass. App.,* or *N. E. 2d* was heard in a state court. Chapter One provides assistance in determining the importance of specific court decisions.

No one will become a legal expert by reading this volume. It is to be hoped, however, that the issues presented here will stimulate thought, cause current practices to be reviewed, and in general provide helpful information to administrators who must cope with a complex legal environment.

Margaret J. Barr
Editor

Margaret J. Barr is vice-president for student affairs at Northern Illinois University, DeKalb. She was assistant vice-president for student affairs at Northern Illinois University and associate and assistant dean of students at the University of Texas, Austin. She is president-elect of the American College Personnel Association, in which she has been active for many years. Her publications have appeared in journals, books, and monographs.

In an increasingly litigious society, colleges and universities
are not immune from legal challenge. The student affairs
administrator needs a basic understanding of the
legal system.

Legal Constraints on
Colleges and Universities

Margaret J. Barr

Almost every decision or action of the student affairs administrator today has legal implications. This certainly has not always been the case. When student affairs administrators functioned under the doctrine of in loco parentis, decisions regarding students and student life were rarely challenged. When colleges and universities were less complex environments, the chance that an institution would have to defend its actions in a courtroom was remote. Increasingly, however, our society uses legal challenges to settle differences, and colleges and universities are not immune from this trend (VanAlystene, 1968). That reality, coupled with a fundamental change in interpretation of the arenas in which constitutionally protected rights must be enforced (Wright, 1969), has required student affairs administrators to become aware of the law and to use that awareness as they deal with students, faculty, staff, and members of the community.

Prior to 1965, only thirty-two landmark cases affecting student development in higher education had been adjudicated in the courts (Hammond and Shaffer, 1978). Since that time, litigation involving postsecondary education has increased dramatically. Issues involving student discipline, the student press, admissions standards, liability of administrators in supervision of activities, and provision of health and counseling services have all been litigated. Given the climate of the times, it appears not only prudent but necessary for student affairs professionals to understand the legal implications of what they do.

M. J. Barr (Ed.). *Student Affairs and the Law.* New Directions for
Student Services, no. 22. San Francisco: Jossey-Bass, June 1983.

4

Unfortunately, most student affairs administrators do not have a strong background in the law. Lack of legal knowledge and training can become a formidable barrier when decisions that have legal ramifications are involved. Without such knowledge, poor decisions can be made. It is also possible to go too far in the other direction, by allowing potential legal concerns to outweigh other pressing objectives. One of the requisite skills for successful administration is the ability to sort through conflicting advice and make a decision based on the best information available. This task becomes much more difficult under the pressures of an increasingly litigious society and the pressures to minimize financial risks to an institution.

Since *Tinker* v. *Des Moines Independent School District* (1969), when the Supreme Court declared (*Tinker*, 1969, at 736),"It can hardly be argued that either students or teachers shed their constitutional rights to freedom of speech at the schoolhouse gate," colleges and universities have had to take the United States Constitution into account in their dealings with students, faculty, and staff. However, the sources of legal constraints on the power and authority of institutions of higher education go far beyond the Constitution. They include the applicable state constitution, federal and state statutes, judicial decisions at all levels, regulations of federal and state agencies, and local ordinances. The legal system in the United States in extremely complex, and the administrator must understand it in order to judge the implications of a point of law accurately in any given set of circumstances. This chapter provides a framework that practitioners can use to weigh the potential legal constraints on decisions in student affairs. Here, it must be said that, under some conditions, the effect of legal constraints differs for public and private institutions. The writer will highlight these differences as they appear.

Constitutional Authorities

Both the United States Constitution and the applicable state constitution can have a profound effect on institutions of higher education. Although "The federal constitution has no provision which specifically refers to education," (Kaplin, 1978, p. 10), it does have provisions that directly influence the way in which we conduct our business.

The United States Constitution. The Constitution is the highest authority for law in the United States. No other laws at the federal, state, or local level can conflict with its provisions. The provisions of the First, Fourth, and Fourteenth Amendments are particularly significant for administrators in public colleges and universities. These three amendments provide much of the basis for protection of individual rights in the collegiate setting. The First Amendment states that "Congress shall make no law respecting an establishment of religion or prohibiting the free exercise thereof; or abridging the freedom of speech, or of the press, or the right of the people peacably to assemble and to petition the Government for a redress of grievances" (U.S. CONST. art. I). A

number of cases based on constitutionally protected rights have been successfully litigated; these cases are described elsewhere in this sourcebook.

The Fourth Amendment provides protection against "unreasonable
searches and seizures" (U.S. CONST. art. IV). It has had a profound effect on
the restructuring of residence hall policies. Enforcement of the Fourteenth
Amendment, which provides for equal protection under the law and requires
due process of law for the denial of "life, liberty, or property" (U.S. CONST. art.
XIV), has required massive restructuring of many judicial codes and internal
grievance procedures in colleges and universities.

There is a significant difference between the influence of these constitutional guarantees on public and private institutions. As Kaplin (1978, p. 20)
notes, institutions and their officers are fully subject to the constraints of the
federal Constitution, whereas private institutions and their officers are not.
This is true because, under the law, public institutions operate as an arm of
the state or government, and as governmental entities they are fully subject to
the federal Constitution. Actions taken by public institutions or their officers
are legally defined as *state action* and are thus subject to the federal Constitution. Under certain conditions, the actions of private institutions and their
officers may also be defined as state action and the federal Constitution will
also apply.

If federal or state money is involved, if the institution acts as an agent
of the state in providing a particular service, or if the institution performs a
function that the government generally holds responsibility for in one form or
another, then private institutions can be subject to all constitutional constraints
on their actions. Kaplin (1978, pp. 18–33) explains the circumstances under
which private institutions are fully subject to constitutional constraints. Because this issue is very complex, student affairs administrators in private institutions should seek legal advice before making decisions that may abrogate the
constitutional rights of students or employees.

State Constitutions. For public institutions, the applicable state constitution can have a very real and direct influence on their governance structure,
their power, and authority. Through the residual powers of the federal Constitution, which delegates certain powers to the federal government and cedes all
others to the states and the people, higher education institutions come primarily under state control (Alexander and Solomon, 1972, p. 42). In Arizona,
California, Colorado, Georgia, Idaho, Michigan, Minnesota, Nevada and
Oklahoma, the state constitution provides constitutional autonomy for the
state university (Hofstadter and Smith, 1961). When a constitutionally autonomous institution is established, the control exercised by the state legislature
and other state agencies over its internal operation diminishes. However, even
a constitutionally autonomous university faces some limitations on its autonomy. These limitations involve the appropriation of funds, the general police
power of the state, and other provisions of some constitutions pertaining to the
legislative, executive, and judicial branches (Glenny and Daglish, 1973).

Constitutionally autonomous institutions are the exception rather than the rule in public higher education. Although the constitutions of twenty-seven states make explicit reference to higher education, autonomy is not guaranteed in all cases (Hofstadter and Smith, 1961).

Whether the state constitution makes explicit reference to the state university or not, other provisions can greatly influence both private and public institutions. Under the general police powers reserved for the state, state governments have assumed great responsibility for regulating both private and public higher education (Kaplin, 1978, p. 372). Such regulation can take the form of coordination of higher education, financial regulations, regulation of powers of university police, or licensing requirements. Specific statutes vary from state to state, but both private and public institutions are bound by them. The basis for the exercise of such statutory authority is the provisions of the state constitution.

Judicial Authorities

All courts, including the Supreme Court of the United States, have three essential functions: They settle controversies by applying appropriate laws or principles to a specific set of facts, they construe or interpret enactments of the legislature, and they determine the constitutionality of enactments of the legislature (Alexander and Solomon, 1972, p. 8). The force of any judicial decision depends on the jurisdiction of the deciding court.

Federal Court System. The federal court system consists of a Supreme Court, courts of appeal, special federal courts, and district courts. Each federal district court is a one-judge trial court; its decisions are reported in the *Federal Supplement*. Decisions of a district court are binding only in the district in which judgment is rendered. However, such decisions can be used as precedent for decisions in other federal districts or by courts of appeals. District court decisions can be appealed directly to the appropriate federal court of appeals and, in some special cases, directly to the United States Supreme Court (Kaplin, 1978, p. 15).

Eleven federal districts make up the federal court of appeals. Each district is called a *circuit*. The decisions of the federal court of appeals are reported in the *Federal Reporter*. Each circuit serves as an intermediate appellate court, and cases can be appealed as a matter of right to the appropriate federal court of appeals. Ordinarily, cases are heard by a panel of three judges appointed by the circuit's chief justice. In very important cases, all the judges in the circuit can sit *en banc* to render an opinion. The decisions of one circuit are not binding in other circuits or in district courts in other circuits. Decisions of the federal court of appeals are binding within all courts in the circuit, unless they are appealed to the United States Supreme Court.

United States Supreme Court decisions are "binding precedents throughout the country" (Kaplin, 1978, p. 14) in matters concerning federal constitutional issues and federal statutes. There is no right of appeal to the United States Supreme Court. To appeal a circuit court decision, a writ of certiorari must be filed with the Supreme Court. Denial of the writ of certiorari leaves the law as decided by the circuit court of appeals for that circuit. It does not change the law in other circuits or districts not affected by the original decision. Decisions of the United States Supreme Court are reported in the *United States Reports*.

Most cases bearing on postsecondary education that reach federal courts involve litigation of federal statutes or actions that are alleged to be in conflict with the federal Constitution. Astute administrators in public and private institutions should keep abreast of decisions in federal courts outside their own circuit or district. Such decisions can serve as a bellwether for shifts in interpretation of the law. Finally, case law provides the basis of many legal constraints facing higher education.

State Court Systems. Although there are certain similarities between state court systems, each state's system is unique. In general, state court systems are structured like federal courts, with district courts, courts of appeal, and a supreme court. District courts are usually courts of general jurisdiction that have judicial responsibility for a specific geographic area. Decisions of state district courts are binding in the district in which they are rendered, unless they are reversed on appeal. Most states have separate district courts for civil and criminal matters and continue this separation at the appellate level. To illustrate, Texas has no intermediate court of appeals in criminal matters. The Texas Court of Criminal Appeals is equal to the state supreme court in criminal matters. In civil matters, which are of most immediate concern to student affairs administrators, the Court of Civil Appeals serves as intermediate appeal court. Decisions of the Court of Civil Appeals not reversed by the state supreme court are binding for the entire state. Decisions of the state supreme court are final and binding for the entire state.

State court systems can also involve courts with special or limited jurisdiction. For example, Illinois has established a court of claims. The court of claims has original jurisdiction in monetary issues involving the state, including its public colleges and universities. Careful review of the constitutional authority and the statutory support for the state judicial system is needed in order to determine the jurisdiction of the individual courts and the subsequent influence of judicial decisions that emanate from them.

The *National Reporter System* publishes important state court opinions in such regional or state case publications as the *Northwestern Reporter*. As in the federal judicial system, decisions of state courts in other jurisdictions and other states can become the basis for decisions by a court that has jurisdiction over an institution. For this reason, student affairs administrators should remain current on these legal decisions. Young and others (1973) can provide useful information in this regard.

Most cases tried in state courts that can influence student affairs policies and procedures center on tort liability or contractual issues. A tort is a civil wrong, other than a breach of contract, for which a court can permit a damage remedy (Prosser, 1971). Most tort liability claims involve allegations of negligence or defamation of a person's character. Although the fundamental principle in such civil liability cases is one of responsibility to act in a reasonable and fair manner, an adverse decision can result in a monetary judgment against the institution (Aiken, 1976). The chapter by Rhode in this volume illustrates methods of risk management that can reduce civil liability claims against an institution.

Contractual disputes are also litigated in state courts. As a matter of routine, student affairs administrators often sign contracts for employment, entertainment, services, or supplies. Such contracts obligate both parties, and knowledge of the legal ramifications of such contracts is essential. In addition, an emerging body of case law is redefining the relationship between the institution and the student as contractual. (See the chapter by Shur in this volume.) Because both tort liability and contractual disputes can involve institutional financial commitment, legal counsel should be sought to minimize the risk of going to state court on either issue. Whether the institution is private or public, risk management is an essential administrative function.

Statutory Authorities

Three levels of statute must be accounted for in institutional administration: federal statutes, state statutes, and local government ordinances. At all three levels, statutes can have a real and direct effect on the administration of student affairs.

Federal Statutes. The laws of the federal government govern the citizens of all the states, and they must be consistent with the powers reserved for the federal government under the United States Constitution. Since passage of the Morrill Act in 1862, the federal government has become increasingly involved both in subsidizing and regulating institutions of higher education. Many policy decisions encountered by student affairs administrators derive directly from federal statutes and the implementing regulations issued by federal agencies.

Federal statutes cover such diverse areas as military training on campus, disposition of surplus property, construction of facilities, individual privacy, and student financial assistance. The range and diversity of federal statutory involvement in both public and private higher education are immense. For example, three different federal laws prohibit discrimination in federally supported education-related programs. Discrimination on the basis of color, race or national origin is prohibited by Title VI of the Civil Rights Act of 1965. Discrimination on the basis of sex in prohibited by Title IX of the Educational Amendments Act of 1972. Discrimination on the basis of handicap is prohibited by Section 504 of the Rehabilitation Act of 1973. Each statute has spawned many pages of implementing regulations by the federal agencies involved. Proposed implementing regulations for all federal statutes are published in the *Federal Register*, together with invitations to comment. Often the regulations are so detailed, that compliance is difficult or impossible. Student affairs administrators who remain abreast of legislative developments by reading the *Chronicle of Higher Education* or some other publication can take advantage of the opportunity to comment. While it may not be possible to change the regulations, the vigilant administrator can at least make an attempt to mitigate their effect on campus. The three antidiscrimination statutes just described have mandated great changes in the provision of student services. Both private and public institutions can be influenced by these and other federal statutes if federal money is directly or indirectly involved in educational programs.

State Statutes. Both public and private institutions are directly influenced by state law (Moos and Rourke, 1959). Both types of institution must conform to the state's general laws. In addition the power and authority for governance of the institution derives directly from state law. The residual powers of the federal Constitution delegate certain powers to the federal government and cede all others to the state and people. Thus, all higher education institutions come primarily under state control (Alexander and Solomon, 1972, p. 42).

Private institutions usually come under state control through incorporation or chartering and licensure or coordination bodies. All states incorporate or charter private postsecondary institutions, although the specific statutes differ from state to state. As Kaplin (1978, p. 374) notes, "State corporation laws usually do not pose significant problems for postsecondary institutions, since their requirements can usually be met easily and routinely." About two thirds of the states also require licensing, which sets much stricter standards for compliance (Education Commission of the States, 1973). Finally, state-mandated coordination of degree programs, service areas, and financial aid programs can all create another form of state statutory regulation for private institutions.

Both private and public institutions also are subject to regulations of state agencies whose main functions are not education. Such agencies include labor relations boards, unemployment compensation agencies, and mental health licensing agencies. Although private institutions are shielded from much state regulation, they are not immune to regulations derived from the general police power of the state.

As already noted, a state can establish public institutions of higher education either as constitutionally autonomous entities or as statutory institutions. However, "the greater part of law defining the status of public institutions of higher education is legislative rather than constitutional" (Moos and Rourke, 1959, p. 17). A statutory institution is created by the legislature, and it is subject to control by the legislative body. Statutory institutions can be defined as either primary or secondary state agencies (Alexander and Solomon, 1972, p. 46). An institution organized as a primary agency responds directly to the legislature. An institution organized as a secondary agency reports to the legislature through another intermediate agency, such as a state coordinating board. In many states, however, a mixed reporting relationship has evolved whereby institutions report directly to the legislature on some matters and to the intermediate agency on others. Primarily through the weight of academic tradition, some observers feel that statutory institutions enjoy greater autonomy than other state agencies do (Glenny and Daglish, 1973).

Public institutions of higher education are controlled by lay governing boards. The composition of the board, its powers, and procedures for appointment of board members are all governed by state statutes. State statutes also define the range of authority vested in it. The amount of explicit, implied, or inherent power given to the board directly affects the day-to-day operation of the institution. Much of the authority granted to institutional governing boards must necessarily be carried out by administrative officers. The delegation of authority by governing boards to institutional representatives must be consistent with the statutory provisions controlling the power of the governing board.

Local Ordinances. The effect of local ordinances on an institution of higher education is determined in part by the charter or license of the private institution and by the statutory entitlement of the public institution. It is also determined by the statutory entitlement of the municipality or county in which the institution is located and by the specific issues at hand. In general, as part of state government, a state institution has "plenary powers over local government unless restricted by state or federal constitutional provisions" (Thompson, 1976, p. 97). However, the law makes a distinction between governmental functions and proprietary functions in determining the superiority of the state institution over local ordinances regarding general health and safety. Zoning laws, police protection, employment laws, fire protection, and other ordinances must be adhered to by public institutions if the state constitution recognizes municipal home rule. As Meyers (1970, p. 3) notes, "The growing insistence that institutions of higher learning become 'involved' with the communities they serve gives rise to even more relationships which have legal implications." Thus, local ordinances can have great influence on particular situations, and neither public nor private institutions can ignore them. The legal authority of the local government body and the legal authority of the institution must carefully be compared.

Other Sources

For public institutions, an opinion rendered by the state's attorney general can be binding unless the institution successfully challenges it in the courts. Except under unusual circumstances, such as those involving financial aid, private institutions are not usually bound by the opinions of state attorneys general.

Administrative regulations and rules issued by state and federal agencies can also carry the force of law. The preceding section highlighted some concerns in this area. Some agencies, such as labor and human rights agencies, also have the legal right to settle disputes on specific issues. A review of the scope of responsibility of such agencies will indicate whether such power has been vested in them. If it has, they deserve serious legal attention, in order to avoid adjudication by an agency outside the institution. On the federal level, a number of agencies also have binding power to resolve disputes or sanction an institution for noncompliance with agency directives. (The chapter by Rhode in this volume discusses this issue.) In any case, the astute administrator needs to become knowledgeable about such regulations. To be less than knowledgeable invites litigation, possible sanctions, and even forced settlement to any issue.

Conclusion

The legal system of this country is complex. This chapter highlights the main sources of the legal constraints that can influence the administration of student affairs units directly. An understanding of the sources of potential legal challenge to institutional authority can assist student affairs administrators in day-to-day activities. The institution's legal status — private or public, constitutionally autonomous or statutory — provides the basis for action by institutional representatives in routine situations. There is every reason to believe that legal challenges will continue at their present pace. The astute student affairs administrator needs to be aware of the potential sources of such challenges and to develop methods that can avoid legal disputes whenever possible. Other chapters in this sourcebook discuss current legal concerns facing institutions in detail. At times, however, an important principle is at the heart of the dispute. At those times, the only answer is litigation. If the student affairs administrator understands the legal framework in which the institution must operate, then informed choices can be made. One final note: The law is an evolving, changing standard. New statutes and new judicial interpretations can substantially alter the legal framework in which we must operate. The only answer is to keep informed, question internally prior to outside challenge, and seek competent legal advice.

References

Aiken, R. J. "Legal Liabilities in Higher Education: Their Scope and Management." *Journal of College and University Law,* 1976, *3,* (entire issue).
Alexander, K., and Solomon, E. *College and University Law.* Charlottesville, Va.: Michie, 1972.

Education Commission of the States. *Model State Legislation: Report of the Task Force on Model State Legislation for Approval of Postsecondary Institutions and Authorizations to Grant Degrees.* Report No. 39. Washington, D.C.: Education Commission of the States, 1973.

Glenny, L. A., and Daglish, T. K. *Public Universities, State Agencies, and the Law: Constitutional Autonomy in Decline.* Berkeley, Calif.: Center for Research and Development in Higher Education, 1973.

Hammond, E. H., and Shaffer, R. H. *The Legal Foundations of Student Personnel Services in Higher Education.* American College Personnel Assocation (ACPA) Monograph Series. Washington, D.C.: American Personnel & Guidance Association (APGA) Press, 1978.

Hofstadter, R., and Smith, W. (Eds.). *American Higher Education: A Documentary History.* Vol. 1. Chicago: University of Chicago Press, 1961.

Kaplin, W. A. *The Law of Higher Education: Legal Implications of Administrative Decision Making.* San Francisco: Jossey-Bass, 1978.

Meyers, J. H. "Conduct of Enterprises." In A. Knowles (Ed.), *Handbook of College and University Administration.* New York: McGraw-Hill, 1970.

Moos, M., and Rourke, F. *The Campus and the State.* Baltimore: Johns Hopkins Press, 1959.

Prosser, W. L. *Handbook on the Law of Torts.* (4th ed.) St. Paul, Minn.: West Publishing, 1971.

Thompson, J. *Policymaking in American Public Education.* Englewood Cliffs, N.J.: Prentice-Hall, 1976.

VanAlystene, W. A. "The Demise of the Right-Privilege Distinction in Constitutional Law." *Harvard Law Review,* 1968, *81,* 1439–1464.

Wright, C. A. "The Constitution On the Campus." *Vanderbilt Law Review,* 1969, *22,* 1027–1088.

Young, D. P., Gehring, D. D., and others (Eds.). *The College Student and the Courts.* Asheville, N.C.: College Administration Publications, 1973, with quarterly supplements.

Margaret J. Barr is vice-president for student affairs at Northern Illinois University, DeKalb, Illinois. She is president-elect of the American College Personnel Association.

The federal Constitution applies with full force on the college campus.
Fundamental fairness is a necessary condition of due process for
students in disciplinary proceedings.

What Process Is Due?

Frank P. Ardaiolo

The Fourteenth Amendment of the United States Constitution declares that
no state shall "deprive any person of life, liberty, or property, without due process of law." Due process is difficult to define precisely, because it is a flexible
concept related to time and circumstances. In the words of the Supreme Court
in *Cafeteria and Restaurant Workers* v. *McElroy* (1961), "the nature of due process
negates any concept of inflexible procedures universally applicable to every
imaginable situation, and it is not a technical conception with a fixed content
unrelated to time, place, and circumstance."

As a legal concept, due process has been held to have two dimensions,
substantive and procedural (Alexander and Solomon, 1972). Substantive due
process speaks to the nature and purpose of rules and regulations of institutions. Courts have held that a government cannot deprive a person of life,
liberty, or property by an unreasonable act without a legitimate purpose.
Procedural due process speaks to the process of judicial decision making.
Obviously, it lies at the heart of the question, What process is due?

It may be of some comfort to the harried student affairs administrator
in a disciplinary situation involving a student that the question "What process
is due this student?" has been asked since 1200 A.D. At that time, organized
learning was associated with moral development and the church. In Paris, a
group of clerical students was involved in a brawl with citizens of the community, and the students were arrested by secular authorities. In sorting out the
conflict between town and gown, King Philip Augustus, bowing to Church

M. J. Barr (Ed.). *Student Affairs and the Law.* New Directions for
Student Services, no. 22. San Francisco: Jossey-Bass, June 1983.

14

pressure, granted the students of the nascent University of Paris their first privilege when he decreed: "Neither our provost nor our judges shall lay hands on a student for any offense whatever, nor shall they place him in our prison, unless such a crime has been committed by the student that he ought to be arrested. And in that case, our judges shall arrest him on the spot, without striking him at all, unless he resists, and shall hand him over to the ecclesiastical judge, who ought to guard him in order to satisfy us and the one suffering the injury" (Wieruszowski, 1966, p. 137). The responsibility for disciplining students has remained with colleges and universities for the last 800 years. However, the question of what is required to guarantee due process continues to be asked on the campus and in the courts.

This chapter undertakes to answer that question by examining current discipline issues and applicable case law. The principle of fundamental fairness will be discussed in detail, and examples of its application to discipline and academic procedures will be given. Finally, some standards for student affairs administrators in examining current procedures and practices will be suggested.

Fundamental Fairness

The evolution of the legal relationship between students and postsecondary institutions can be understood as emanating from the sources of legal constraints described in Chapter One. These sources of legal constraints continually interact with the decisions reached by courts at all levels of the American judicial system. In general, court decisions that affect the student affairs administrator relate to the administrator's functional responsibility for student discipline (Dannells, 1977).

The doctrine of in loco parentis comes from common law, the judicial interpretations inherited from England by the American colonies. This doctrine, which governed the American college view of discipline for many years, holds that college authorities act in the place of parents. This allows institutions to make and enforce any rule concerning the moral, physical, and intellectual betterment of students that parents would make.

The civil rights movement of the 1960s forced both a legal and a philosophic change. Constitutional law, which afforded students rights as citizens under the United States Constitution, came to predominate. No longer could the universities, through administrators, act in place of students' parents; rather, the Constitution guaranteed students certain due process rights, and it was the responsibility of the administrator to see that these rights were provided.

Today, the scene is changing again, as many current cases appeal to contract law. (See Chapter Three in this volume.) Student consumers are demanding better information, choice, hearing, and safety as partners in their contractual relationship with postsecondary institutions. This shift to a view of the relationship between student and institution as contractual in nature provides a new framework for the student-university relationship (Ardaiolo, 1978). The judicial system appears to be adopting this new contractual emphasis in part because many of the issues regarding what process is due within the constitutional context seem to have been resolved to the satisfaction of the current Supreme Court.

Constitutional Issues. The death knell of the judicial doctrine of in loco parentis on college campuses was sounded in 1961. A series of rulings by federal courts established that students do not "shed their constitutional rights... at the schoolhouse gate" (*Tinker* v. *Des Moines Independent School District*, 1969). Depending on the situation and the case at hand, the United States Constitution was applied by the courts to the student-institution relationship. Thus, the First Amendment protection of speech, press, and religion; the Fourth Amendment protection against unreasonable searches and seizures; and the Fourteenth Amendment guarantees of due process and equal protection came into play, and student affairs administrators were forced to react accordingly.

The freedoms and liberties guaranteed by the Constitution protect individual students as citizens from infringement by the U.S. Congress and state governments. As an arm of government, the public postsecondary institution is subject to the same constitutional limitations. And, when it can be shown to the satisfaction of a court that a private institution functions in such a way that state action is present, then it, too, is subject to the same constitutional requirements (Alexander and Solomon, 1972).

All these requirements apply to public institutions. Their applicability to private institutions varies with the substance of the issue and the specific institution. It could be argued from a policy standpoint that private institutions should observe all the procedural requirements that apply to public institutions, as this would serve to insulate them from court review. Therefore, this chapter draws no legal distinction between public and private institutions.

Chronological review of the most important federal case law shows that the term *due process* as applied to the student-university relationship and to the disciplinary and academic processes involved has been understood to mean fundamental fairness. While many authors have traced and interpreted these judicial developments, the works by Kaplin (1978), Young (1976), and Young and Gehring (1976) are the most relevant for college administrators. The concept of fundamental fairness can be understood and operationalized in the collegiate setting in a way that both preserves the educative aspects of student development and does much to protect student affairs administrators from judicial intrusion.

In 1961, a landmark decision (*Dixon* v. *Alabama State Board of Education*, 1961) established the right of students at a state institution to notice and a hearing in disciplinary proceedings in which suspension or expulsion was a possibility. The court held that "In the disciplining of college students... [the university should exercise] at least the fundamental principles of fairness by giving the accused students notice of the charges and an opportunity to be heard in their own defense" (*Dixon*, 1961, at 150).

The court discussed specific guidelines that could enable the institution to meet the principle of fundamental fairness in great detail. These guidelines include notice, with an outline of specific charges; a fair and impartial hearing; the names of witnesses; the content of witnesses' statements; and the opportunity to speak in one's own defense. Finally, the court held that "the results and findings of the hearing should be presented in a report open to the student's inspection. If these rudimentary elements of fair play are followed in a case of misconduct of this particular type, we feel the requirements of due process of law will have been fulfilled" (*Dixon*, 1961, p. 157).

Due v. *Florida A. & M. University* (1963), a case involving campus discipline proceedings for students convicted off campus on contempt of court charges, is also significant. *Due* established that the standard for procedural due process in disciplinary hearings is one of fundamental fairness and reasonableness.

In *Connelly* v. *University of Vermont* (1965), where a medical student received a failing grade for make-up work, the court made a distinction between disciplinary dismissal and academic dismissal (Mancuso, 1977). Disciplinary dismissal was defined as arising from violations of prescribed conduct. Academic dismissal was defined as based on academic evaluation. *Connelly* established the principle that a student must demonstrate arbitrariness, capriciousness, or bad faith before a court can interfere in an academic matter.

Esteban v. *Central Missouri State College* (1969) established specifications for fairness in student disciplinary proceedings, but it also recognized the unique context and constraints at each institution. The court outlined the following nine procedures (Kaplin, 1978): a written charge statement, made available at least ten days before the hearing; a hearing for the charged student before those with power to suspend or expel; an opportunity for the charged student to review the information to be submitted at the hearing in advance; the right of the charged student to bring counsel to furnish advice but not to question witnesses; the right of the charged student to present a version of the facts through personal and written statements, including the statements of witnesses; an opportunity for the charged student to hear all information presented against him and to question adverse witnesses personally (not through counsel); a determination of the facts of the case based solely on what is presented at the hearing by the authority that holds the hearing; a written statement of the findings of fact; and the right of the charged student to make a record of the hearing at his own expense.

In *Gaspar* v. *Bruton* (1975), which dealt with a case involving academic dismissal at a state school, the court recognized the property interest of the Fourteenth Amendment. However, it stopped far short of the due process standards established in disciplinary dismissals, stating "We hold that school authorities, in order to satisfy due process prior to termination or suspension of a student for deficiencies in meeting academic performance, need only to advise that student with regard to such deficiencies in any form. All that is required is that the student must be made aware prior to termination of his failure or impending failure to meet these standards" (*Gaspar,* 1975, at 843).

In another U.S. Court of Appeals decision in that same year, the court extended due process protection to the student in an academic dismissal case, because the university notified a professional association of the student's "lack of intellectual ability or insufficient preparation"; this stigmatized him, so that he was deprived of a "significant interest in liberty and property" covered by the Fourteenth Amendment (*Greenhill* v. *Bailey*, 1975). The court held that Greenhill should have been notified of his alleged deficiency and that he should have had an opportunity to answer such allegations personally. The landmark decision by the Supreme Court in the case of *Board of Curators of the University of Missouri* v. *Horowitz* (1978) has placed limitations on the application of procedural due process requirements to academic dismissals. The court ruled that the due process clause does not requires a hearing before the appropriate decision-making body when a student is dismissed for academic reasons, if the student has been informed of the academic deficiencies in question and of the danger they pose to timely graduation before it makes the "careful and deliberate" decision to dismiss her. In reaching this decision, the court assumed that the student had a property or liberty interest at stake. Noting that there is a dichotomy between academic evaluations and traditional disciplinary determinations of misconduct, the court stated: "Like the decision of an individual professor as to the proper grade for a student in his course, the determination whether to dismiss a student for academic reasons requires an expert evaluation of cumulative information and is not readily adapted to the procedural tools of judicial or administrative decision making... Under such circumstances, we decline to ignore the historic judgment of educators and thereby formalize the academic dismissal process by requiring a hearing" (*Board of Curators*, 1978, at 79).

The Academic/Disciplinary Sanction Dichotomy. As the cases just cited show, it is clear that the Supreme Court perceives a difference in the procedural due process requirements for students facing academic sanctions and the due process requirements for students facing disciplinary sanctions. A number of articles have dealt with the legal implications of the *Board of Curators* decision (Edwards and Nordin, 1981, p. 70). Of special concern are the court's seemingly restrictive view of the liberty and property rights of students in similar educational institutions and the apparent retreat of students' corresponding due process rights that the decision signals (Mass, 1980). Dessem (1978) interprets the decision to signify that many academic decisions will no longer be subject to federal judicial scrutiny and that institutions may even be allowed to ignore their own procedures in certain instances. He points out that many state constitutions may now afford students more due process protection than the federal Constitution, since appears that the current Supreme Court is restricting application of the Fourteenth Amendment.

The dichotomy established in the *Horowitz* case may be very difficult to apply in fact. The court seems to say that significantly less due process is required when academic evaluative judgments, such as grading or determinations of students' suitability for a profession, are involved than in a discipline case, when fact-finding seeks to establish whether a student violated a rule of behavior. As Kaplin (1978, p. 248) points out, it can be argued that, even in the *Horowitz* case, fact-finding was present, for the justices of the Supreme Court split on the issue, with five judges applying the academic label, two judges applying the disciplinary label or arguing that no label was appropriate, and two judges refusing to apply either label or to decide "whether such a distinction is relevant."

While there is still some confusion about what due process, other than "careful and deliberate" decision making, is required in academic evaluation cases, La Morte and Meadows (1979, p. 197) suggest that "students have been treated fairly when they understand as precisely as possible what is required of them, receive an explanation as soon as possible why they are not meeting these requirements and of what steps might be taken to correct their noncompliance, and are aware beforehand of the possible outcomes of their actions or nonactions pertaining to academic matters."

Discipline as Teaching. The teaching process is unique. Courts have long recognized this, and as a result, they have been extremely reluctant to substitute their judgment for that of academic experts (Hollander, 1978). Student affairs administrators must emphasize that they are the academic experts in the matter of discipline, for it is an important dimension of both student development (Greenleaf, 1978; Ostroth and Hill, 1978) and liberal education. As Brubacher (1977, p. 82) states, liberal education must "be concerned with habituation in moral conduct as well as with its theoretical analysis. It must educate the whole person, the appetites as well as intellect."

Discipline truly involves teaching. A court that identified sixteen lawful missions of tax-supported higher education (*General Order on Judicial Standards of Procedures and Substance in Review of Student Discipline in Tax-Supported Institutions of Education*, 1968) included the following: "(1) To develop students to well-rounded maturity, physically, socially, emotionally, spiritually, intellectually, and vocationally; (2) to develop, refine, and teach ethical and cultural values; and (3) to teach the practice of excellence in thought, behavior, and performance" (*General Order*, 1968, p. 133).

The significant federal court cases reviewed here all illustrate that what the federal Constitution legally requires in student discipline cases is a policy of fundamental fairness that governs all procedures. Discipline is a functional aspect of education, and the courts have been most reluctant to enter this domain.

Student affairs administrators do themselves and students a disservice if they overreact to due process requirements. A judicial process on campus that mimics a genuine adversarial court hearing is not required and only invites judicial review of the process. If we believe that student discipline has educational value, then we must adhere to that belief in developing sound judicial practices. It must not be forgotten that, many times, the students who violate institutional standards are the students who can benefit most from disciplinary measures that can assist in their cognitive, ethical, and interpersonal growth. As the *General Order* declared, "the attempted analogy of student discipline to criminal proceedings against adults and juveniles is not sound" (*General Order*, 1968, p. 147).

This is not to say that one does not have to be expert in administering the educational disciplinary process. There has been much litigation in this area, and student affairs administrators must be prepared to balance the needs and rights of students, faculty, and the institution and do so in a way that enables students to learn and the academic community to prosper (Rutherford and Osway, 1981). While certain authors (Caruso, 1978; Ostroth and Hill, 1978; Tice, 1976) have discussed the specifically educational aspects of establishing this needed balance, it must be emphasized, first, that discipline is an integral part of the teaching process and of student development in postsecondary education and, second, that the courts, for the most part, have established fundamental fairness as the basic parameter of students' constitutional rights.

Fundamental fairness can be defined as that which is reasonable, impartial, and free from bias. As many of the cases just cited show, the courts have defined fundamental fairness as that which is not arbitrary, capricious, or done in bad faith. Arbitrariness occurs when actions are taken without cause in an unrestrained or unreasonable way. Capriciousness indicates that an action or finding is without rational basis. It should be easy for student affairs professionals to understand these commonsense definitions and to articulate them in policies and procedures for dealing with students. We should, therefore, let fundamental fairness be our guide and avoid using the elusively defined term *due process*.

Administration of Student Discipline

The parameters of the application of constitutionally protected student due process rights in public postsecondary institutions as determined by the Supreme Court in the *Horowitz* case are stated in the preceding section. The knowledgeable student affairs administrator knows, however, that a number of other significant aspects in the administration of student discipline must also be considered, for lesser federal courts continue to review specific aspects of student discipline. Buchanan (1978) provides a concise overview, Kaplin (1978) is most valuable, and Young and Gehring (1976) are indispensable in keeping abreast of case law and current issues. The following synopsis of case law, which draws heavily from these three sources, is provided to illustrate these issues.

Specificity of Rules and Regulation. In developing rules of conduct or regulations of performance, administrators must be careful to avoid vague wording, for enforcement of vagueness can violate due process. In *Soglin* v. *Kauffman* (1969), the term *misconduct* was held to violate due process as a standard for disciplinary action. The general standard for the degree of specificity required was set in *Sword* v. *Fox* (1971). Under that decision, the adequate standard "conveys sufficiently definite warning as to the proscribed conduct when measured by common understanding and practice" and allows a student to prepare an adequate defense against the charge, as held in *Scott* v. *Alabama State Board of Education* (1969).

For example, in *Lowery* v. *Adams* (1972), the court held that the following rule, while not as precise as it could be, was still constitutional: "any disruptive or disorderly conduct which interferes with the rights and opportunities of those who attend the university for the purpose for which the university exists — the right to utilize and enjoy facilities provided to obtain an education" (*Lowery*, 1972, at 446). However, a regulation at Jackson State University that permitted only "activities of a wholesome nature" was held to be unconstitutionally vague and overbroad (*Shamloo* v. *Mississippi State Board of Trustees, Etc.*, 1980). The court pointed out that the regulation was so vague that different university administrators could interpret it in different, arbitrary, and discriminatory ways.

Composition of Hearing Boards. In an attempt to provide "representation with regard to race and sex on the student judicial board" (*Uzzell* v. *Friday*, 1980, at 1117), the University of North Carolina at Chapel Hill set up a quota system assuring that the composition of the board was based upon the sex and race of the charged student. This quota system was held to violate both the Fourteenth Amendment and the Civil Rights Act, because the quotas violated other students' rights solely on the basis of race. This is not a final ruling, because the case is still under appeal.

However, the right of universities to specify the composition of the hearing boards has been upheld. In *Sill* v. *Penn State University* (1970), the university was even allowed not to use the existing judicial board but to appoint a special disciplinary panel of distinguished private citizens. Similarly, in *Winnick* v. *Manning* (1972), where the sole judge in a disciplinary hearing was an administrator from the dean of students office that had initiated the proceedings, the court held that procedural due process had not been violated.

Off-Campus Incidents Resulting in On-Campus Hearings. It was established in the early 1960s that institutions have the authority to initiate on-campus disciplinary hearings that follow normal procedures solely because students have been convicted of crimes against criminal or civil law (*Due* v. *Florida A. & M. University*, 1963). Universities may also proceed with on-campus disciplinary hearings without waiting for the result of off-campus criminal proceedings for acts that occurred on campus without fear of violating student constitutional rights, particularly the right against self-incrimination (*Furutani* v. *Ewigleben*, 1969). However, institutions must avoid regulations that require automatic disciplinary sanctions for off-campus convictions without providing students with a hearing or with an opportunity for students to demonstrate that they are not a threat to the institution (*Paine* v. *Board of Regents of University of Texas System*, 1972).

The key in deciding whether to charge a student with violation of university rules for an off-campus act is the determination that that act has some detrimental impact on the educational mission of the university (*Krasnow* v. *Virginia Polytechnic Institute and State University*, 1976). To cite from the influential *General Order* (1968): "In the field of discipline, scholastic and behavioral, an institution may establish any standards reasonably relevant to the lawful missions, processes, and functions of the institution... Standards so established may apply to student behavior on and off the campus when relevant to any lawful mission, process, or function of the institution" (*General Order*, 1968, p. 145).

Interim or Emergency Suspension. On occasion, student affairs administrators are faced with an immediate situation the facts of which indicate that a student's continued presence on campus constitutes a clear and convincing danger to the normal functions of the institution, to property, to others, or to the student himself. Case law (*Stricklin* v. *Regents of University of Wisconsin*, 1969; *Buck* v. *Carter*, 1970; *Woodruff* v. *West Virginia Board of Regents*, 1971; and *Gardenshire* v. *Chalmers*, 1971) has established that administrators have the authority in such situations to suspend the student immediately on an emergency basis until a regular hearing can be held. Students should be provided a preliminary hearing before the suspension takes effect, unless it is impossible or unreasonably difficult to accord it. In this situation, notice outlining the reasons for the action should be given to the student, and a place and time should be set for the regular hearing. It is suggested that the regular hearing be held within fifteen days of the original action.

Mandatory Psychiatric Withdrawal. Recently, many campuses have become concerned about the proper response to students who exhibit mental disturbance and about the legality of procedures utilized in the mandatory withdrawal of such students for psychiatric reasons (Bernard and Bernard, 1980; Zirkel and Bargerstock, 1980). In particular, university administrators have asked whether Section 504 of the Rehabilitation Act of 1973, as amended, which prohibits discrimination against the handicapped—who, under its definition, include those suffering from "psychological disorder, such as emotional or mental illness"—applies to separation proceedings for students who exhibit mental disturbance.

Case law on this particular issue is silent for public institutions. In a comprehensive review and analysis of related case law, Pavela (1982) argues convincingly that public institutions should rely on a properly drafted disciplinary code. Such a code should not use vague and ambiguous language in standards that prohibit such behavior as "disturbed," "of concern to others," or "abnormal"; the code should rely instead on judgment based on the observable facts of prohibited behavior. Pavela describes possible procedural standards that an institution that believes that the disciplinary process is ill suited for dealing with such instances could adopt. Pavela believes that only in instances of severe mental disorder, where a student lacks the capacity to respond to charges or where the student does not know the nature and quality of the act in question, should the student be withdrawn and referred to an approved mental health facility for psychiatric observation and evaluation. Until future case law provides further guidance, this cautionary approach appears to be the best.

Right to Counsel. The role of counsel for the student charged in a campus judicial proceeding has been well outlined (*Gabrilowitz* v. *Newman,* 1978). Two student affairs administrators involved in *Gabrilowitz* (Weisinger and Crafts, 1979; Weisinger, 1981) make it clear that this limited right of students is applicable only when the charged student faces criminal and university disciplinary charges stemming from the same incident. The institution is allowed to proceed before the criminal trial takes place, and the student is allowed to have an outside attorney present only to act in a limited and passive role, which does not include presenting a traditional legal defense. This limited and passive role allows outside counsel only to directly assist the student. The student or a chosen faculty, student or staff advisor who is not an attorney conducts the direct defense to the hearing board. Counsel has an opportunity to protect the student from self-incrimination and to observe the proceedings firsthand in preparation for the pending criminal trial. However, where a university prosecutes students before the appropriate hearing authority using an attorney or even a senior law student, the charged students have a right to be fully represented by counsel in order to preserve fundamental fairness (*French* v. *Bashful,* 1969).

Policy Guidelines

In this chapter, the constitutional context for discipline has been set, and certain troublesome issues have been reviewed. Such information is sterile, however, unless it is combined with suggestions for good practice based on managerial and educational experiences. This section presents some legal and policy guidelines that should be considered by those who wish to develop a fundamentally fair discipline system.

Clearly Articulated Educational Philosophy. Since the time of King Philip Augustus, discipline has been a responsibility of educational institutions as we know them. This educational inheritance should be understood and clearly stated so that the court fully understands that the procedures followed were developed in good faith as part of the lawful educational mission of the university. Additionally, student affairs administrators must be able to articulate how these procedures contribute to the educational process of student development, for courts are most hesitant about intruding in matters in which they are not expert.

Specificity of Rules. The regulations of the institution should be presented in such a way that their relationship to the educational mission is readily apparent. The regulations should be specific enough that students can know their obligations in all situations. The rules should not attempt to be exhaustive, for this can be provocative to students adept at exploitation, and it can allow the system to break down under legalisms. The regulations should explain the distinction between criminal laws and institutional rules, and they should allow the university to deal with criminal arrest on and off campus.

Authority and Responsibility. The authority to act and the responsibility for action should be vested in the same administrative office. If authority and responsibility are split, the system can become unmanageable. Discipline is complex, and well-intentioned intrusions by members of the academic community can paralyze an elaborate check-and-balance system. Additionally, a mechanism should be established that allows both for timely modification of the system as case law and experience dictate and for meaningful input from students, faculty, and administrators.

Choice of Hearing. While no legal requirement specifies who can conduct a hearing, experience suggests that charged students should be given a choice between an administrative hearing and a board hearing in order to maximize both the educational impact and the appearance of fairness to the charged students. The educational aspects of student peer review should also be encouraged. However, if peer review is provided, the student board must be properly trained and supervised in order to guarantee that the process is both educationally meaningful and legally sufficient.

Fundamentally Fair Procedures. While some lower courts have suggested specific hearing requirements that go beyond the notice and hearing required by the Supreme Court, the following can be suggested as fundamentally fair procedures: written notice of the alleged violation, opportunity for a hearing with time to prepare for it, confidentiality of proceedings, opportunity to hear all information presented and to question all who present information, opportunity to present information on one's own behalf, right to have legal counsel present to advise the student, opportunity to challenge the objectivity of judges, and a timely decision.

Appeal. An opportunity to appeal a decision is not legally required. However, an opportunity to appeal is suggested, in order both to maximize fairness and to correct any defects of the original hearing. The grounds for appeal should be outlined. These grounds could include original decision contrary to the facts, availability of new information, procedural violations, or excessive severity of the sanction.

Educational Sanctions. Once the hearing process has established the responsibility for violation of a rule, the sanction assigned to a student should be described and administered in an educational way, so that its teaching potential is enhanced. Requiring students who violate institutional rules to explore the impact of their actions on victims, to prepare research papers on the meaning of education, or to attend special programs, such as an alcohol education seminar, should all be considered.

Emergency Suspension. For situations that pose an immediate threat, the institution should outline procedures for a policy of emergency or interim suspension before a regular hearing can be held. These procedures should include a policy for dealing with the profoundly emotionally disturbed. Policy guidelines in these areas minimize the potential for arbitrary or capricious decisions by administrators and outline the protections afforded to students.

Unified Academic and Social Discipline System. As the review of case law indicates, there can still be some legal confusion over whether a specific violation is of an academic or a disciplinary nature, which raises a question about the corresponding appropriate procedures. Clearly, charges of cheating and plagiarism are very similar to violations of social standards, and they should be treated procedurally in the same manner in a unified administrative system that preserves the teacher's authority to assign grades, maintains institutional efficiency, and assures procedural correctness. In academic evaluative situations that could lead to a student's dismissal and which the facts are disputed, it is suggested that procedures with constitutional safeguards similar to social discipline be adopted as a matter of policy to protect the student from arbitrary, capricious, or bad faith decision making.

Summary

Student discipline has evolved through a series of legal interpretations derived from common law and constitutional law. It has been firmly established that discipline is an aspect of the lawful teaching and student development functions of postsecondary institutions. The courts have held that the disciplinary process requires only fundamental fairness, as long as the disciplinary process as part of the teaching and educational mission of the university. As a matter of common law, the courts have adopted a doctrine of academic abstention, by which they refuse to interfere in the basic academic process of teaching and evaluating students (Edwards and Nordin, 1979). In dealing with students, the constitutional parameters of due process have been defined so that administrators faced with a disciplinary encounter who ask, "What process is due?" can answer that the institution must provide procedures governing students that are fundamentally fair.

References

Alexander, K., and Solomon, E. L. *College and University Law.* Charlottesville, Va.: Michie, 1972.

Ardaiolo, F. P. "Educational Consumer Protection at Indiana University, Bloomington." Unpublished doctoral dissertation, Indiana University, 1978.

Bernard, M. L., and Bernard, J. L. "Institutional Responses to Suicidal Student: Ethical and Legal Considerations." *Journal of College Student Personnel,* 1980, *21* (2), 109–113.

Brubacher, J. S. *On the Philosophy of Higher Education.* San Francisco: Jossey-Bass, 1977.

Buchanan, E. T. "Student Disciplinary Proceedings in Collegiate Institutions: Substantive and Procedural Due Process." In E. H. Hammond and R. H. Shaffer (Eds.), *The Legal Foundations of Student Personnel Services in Higher Education.* Washington, D.C.: American College Personnel Association, 1978.

Caruso, R. G. "The Professional Approach to Student Discipline in the Years Ahead." In E. H. Hammond and R. H. Shaffer (Eds.), *The Legal Foundations of Student Personnel Services in Higher Education.* Washington, D.C.: American College Personnel Association, 1978.

Dannells, M. "Discipline." In W. T. Packwood (Ed.), *College Student Personnel Services.* Springfield, Ill.: Thomas, 1977.

Dessem, R. L. "Academic Versus Judicial Expertise." *Ohio State Law Journal,* 1978, *39* (476), 977–996.

Edwards, H. T., and Nordin, V. D. *Higher Education and the Law.* Cambridge, Mass.: Institute for Educational Management, 1979.

Edwards, H. T., and Nordin, V. D. *Higher Education and the Law: 1981 Cumulative Supplement.* Cambridge, Mass.: Institute for Educational Management, 1981.

Greenleaf, E. A. "The Relationship of Legal Issues and Procedures to Student Development." In E. H. Hammond and R. H. Shaffer (Eds.), *The Legal Foundations of Student Personnel Services in Higher Education.* Washington, D.C.: American College Personnel Association, 1978.

Hollander, P. A. *Legal Handbook for Educators.* Boulder, Colo.: Westview Press, 1978.

Kaplin, W. A. *The Law of Higher Education: Legal Implications of Administrative Decision Making.* San Francisco: Jossey-Bass, 1978.

La Morte, M. W., and Meadows, R. B. "Educationally Sound Due Process in Academic Affairs." *Journal of Law and Education,* 1979, *8,* 197–214.

Mancuso, J. H. "Academic Challenges in the Courts." In J. S. Stark (Ed.), *The Many Faces of Educational Consumerism.* Lexington, Mass.: Heath, 1977.

Mass, M. A. "Due Process Rights of Students: Limitations on *Goss* v. *Lopez*: A Retreat Out of the Thicket." *Journal of Law and Education,* 1980, *9,* 449–462.

Ostroth, D. D., and Hill, D. E. "The Helping Relationship in Student Discipline." *NASPA Journal,* 1978, *16* (2), 33–39.

Pavela, G. "Therapeutic Paternalism and the Misuse of Mandatory Psychiatric Withdrawals of Campus." *Journal of College and University Law,* 1982, *9* (2), 101–147.

Rutherford, D. G., and Osway, L. G. "Academic Misconduct: The Due Process Rights of Students." *NASPA Journal,* 1981, *19* (2), 12–16.

Tice, T. N. *Student Rights, Decision Making, and the Law.* Washington, D.C.: American Association of Higher Education, 1976.

Wieruszowski, H. *The Medieval University.* Princeton, N.J.: Nostrand, 1966.

Weisinger, R., and Crafts, R. "Right to Counsel: Legal and Educational Considerations." *NASPA Journal,* 1979, *17* (2), 27–33.

Weisinger, R. "Right to Counsel Revisited." *NASPA Journal,* 1981, *18* (4), 51–55.

Young, D. P. *The Law and Student in Higher Education.* Topeka, Kans.: National Organization On Legal Problems of Education, 1976.

Young, D. P., and Gehring, D. D. (Eds.). *The College Student and the Courts.* Asheville, N.C.: College Administration Publications, 1973, and quarterly supplements.

Zirkel, P. A., and Bargerstock, C. T. "Two Current Legal Concerns in College Student Affairs: Alcohol Consumption and Psychiatric Separation." *Journal of College Student Personnel,* 1980, *21* (3), 252–256.

Frank P. Ardaiolo is dean of students at the University of Connecticut and National Chair of the American College Personnel Association's Commission on Campus Judicial Affairs and Legal Issues.

Definition of the relationship between the student and the institution
as a contract is a relatively recent legal phenomenon. Catalogues,
private and public statements by officials, and written agreements
may all be enforced as contractual obligations to students and
may be the cause of litigation.

Contractual Relationships

George M. Shur

In 1979, Julie Tichbourne brought a lawsuit against her church, arguing that it had breached its contract with her because courses that she took did not help her with her college classwork, develop her creativity, or raise her IQ test scores as claimed. The jury awarded her $2 million. Is nothing sacred?

Only a few years ago, a lawsuit like the one brought by Ms. Tichbourne would have been dismissed as frivolous by most university administrators. But, since the turn of the century, courts have recognized that the student enjoys certain contractual rights and that the institution has concurrent contractual obligations (*Niedermeyer* v. *Curators of University of Missouri*, 1895). In the last decade, the number of court cases involving institutions of higher education and alleged contractual obligations to students has increased dramatically. Most student affairs administrators do not view the student-institution relationship as contractual in nature. However, since the courts increasingly are using contractual law as a basis for the settlement of claims, prudent administrators must increase their knowledge in this area. This chapter proposes to fill the knowledge gap by presenting an overview of the current status of contract and consumer actions brought by students against educational institutions. In addition, it presents guidelines for development of policies and procedures related to contract law.

Current Issues

Virtually every oral and written contract between the student and the institution becomes a contractual obligation. The findings in a number of

M. J. Barr (Ed.). *Student Affairs and the Law.* New Directions for
Student Services, no. 22. San Francisco: Jossey-Bass, June 1983.

court cases have supported the concept that students no longer need to be passive consumers who pay their tuition and fees but have no legal standing in the courts to ensure that the university will meet legitimate contractual obligations. The first case concerning a student's contractual rights which received serious attention in the courts was *Trustees of Columbia University* v. *Jacobsen* (1959). In a counterclaim to a collection suit brought by the university, the former student listed some fifty claims and asked for $7,000 in damages. His lawsuit was based on a variety of charges of fraud and misrepresentation. The crux of his claim was that the university had made certain written and oral promises that it had failed to keep.

For instance, he claimed that the university had represented that it would teach him "wisdom, truth, character, enlightenment, understanding, justice, liberty, honesty, courage, beauty, and similar virtues and qualities; that it would develop the whole man, maturity, well-roundedness, objective thinking and the like" (*Trustees*, 1959, at 65). Because it had failed to do so, Jacobsen argued, he suffered pecuniary loss. During the course of litigation, Jacobsen cited the university's motto—"In your light we shall see the light"—the inscription over the chapel—"Wisdom dwelleth in the heart of him who hath understanding"—and speeches at alumni dinners. It became clear that his real charge was that Columbia had somehow—fraudulently, deceitfully, and in breach of its reprsentations and promises—failed to teach him wisdom. The court found that wisdom is not a subject that can be taught and that no rational person would accept such a claim from any man or institution.

Although Jacobsen lost the case, it was a beginning. Since the early 1970s, the number of responsible student challenges in the areas of tuition changes, student discipline, admissions, academic dismissal, and academic programs has multiplied. In addition to the contract argument, most of the students have relied on other theories of recovery, such as the tort of misrepresentation, the tort of fraud, and constitutional deprivation. In virtually every case, the written or oral representations of the institution—as contained in course catalogues, syllabi, student handbooks, written rules and regulations, and verbal promises—have provided the basis for the claims. Students have been sustained in the courts many times on representations in handbooks, rules and regulations, and verbal promises by institutional officials. Institutions have generally prevailed in cases related to course catalogues and syllabi.

Students often rely on the college catalogue, which, in these days of declining admissions pools, can contain some incautious prose on the school's programs or advantages. Most institutions have included disclaimers in their catalogues, but these disclaimers are usually set in very small type, and they are not prominently displayed. The presence of these disclaimers is important, but an institution cannot rely on disclaimers for protection. According to Bender (1976), it may just be a matter of time before the Federal Trade Commission seeks to impose the same consumer-based regulations on nonprofit institutions that it places on proprietary schools.

The courts have also looked carefully at the written representations of institutions and at statements by officials in determining the legitimacy of contract claims, as some recent court cases illustrate.

Admissions. Two recent cases point up the necessity for an institution carefully to consider the criteria used in admitting students. In *Steinberg* v. *Chicago Medical School* (1977), an unsuccessful applicant filed suit claiming that the admissions committee had failed to evaluate his application pursuant to the criteria listed in the admissions bulletin. He claimed that a "hidden agenda" of criteria was actually used and that he had satisfied all the published criteria. The medical school filed a motion to dismiss that relied on the traditional discretion accorded to professional schools in making decisions about admissions. But, the Illinois Supreme Court refused to grant the dismissal and gave Steinberg the right to present evidence on his claim.

A more traditional view was taken by the Massachusetts Court in *Donnelly* v. *Suffolk University* (1976), where the court held that giving weight to letters of recommendation from alumni or benefactors of the school was neither a breach of the published admissions criteria nor a violation of state unfair practice and consumer statutes and regulations. The court relied on catalogue language giving Suffolk the broadest possible discretion in setting admissions criteria and in making decisions based on those criteria. This is another case where careful drafting of catalogue language caused a court to defer to the good faith discretion of academic administrators.

Academic Dismissal. Challenges to an institution's right to make academic decisions usually include constitutional claims, contractual claims, or both. Courts recognize that similar standards of judicial review attend, regardless of the formal nature of the claim. A federal court in Texas stated: "A student with a grievance may not. . . transform a. . . court into a sort of educational ombudsman whose function is to review the everyday actions of local school officials. It is difficult to imagine an area of academia more suitable for judicial abstention" (*Keys* v. *Sawyer*, 1973, at 940).

When dealing with professors or with areas of study that are highly technical or that require great expertise, the courts have recognized that even more weight should be given to the judgment of trained professionals. To illustrate, a student of history who is found by faculty to be incapable of developing empathic relations with fellow students or faculty might arguably be allowed to graduate with a degree in history, it being presumed that character or personality problems would not in any way affect the person's competency as an historian, nor would the young historian be in a position where, by sole reason of his training and academic degree, he could adversely affect others. Contrast this with the case of a student in medicine or a medically related field, such as mental health technology, who by reason of training and a degree from an institution of higher education can wreak havoc with the mental or physical well-being of others. In a North Carolina case, *Lai* v. *Board of Trustees of East Carolina University* (1971), a student was barred from enrolling in a student teaching program because he admitted that he smoked marijuana cigarettes. In upholding the decision of East Carolina University, the court found as fact that "As a result of the conference with [the student] in the department, [the faculty] felt they had some serious questions about his character in terms of suitability for teaching" (*Lai*, 1971, at 906). The court further stated that colleges and universities "are entitled to wide discretion in the regulation of the training of their students."

One of the first cases to recognize the necessity of strict standards was *Connelly* v. *University of Vermont* (1965). In this case, the court asked two questions. The first question involved the student's qualifications and his ability to meet academic standards. The court concluded that this was not a matter for judicial review. The second question centered on the motivation of the school authorities for the student's dismissal. Had they acted in an arbitrary or capricious manner? The court held that "a student dismissal motivated by bad faith, arbitrariness, or capriciousness may be actionable" (*Connelly*, 1965, at 906).

A decision by the Washington Supreme Court amply defined arbitrary and capricious action in a case (*McDonald* v. *Hogness*, 1979) involving the University of Washington School of Medicine: "Arbitrary and capricious action of administrative bodies means willful and unreasoning action without consideration and in disregard of facts or circumstances. Where there is room for two opinions, action is not arbitrary or capricious when exercising honesty and upon due consideration, even though it may be believed that an erroneous conclusion has been reached" (*McDonald*, 1979, at 717). As a trial judge in Maine stated, "No one has a right to expect decisions to be always correct, only that they be fairly, thoughtfully, and legally arrived at" (*Robertson* v. *Haaland,* 1977).

In *Gasper* v. *Bruton* (1975), the U.S. Court of Appeals again recognized: "The court may grant relief as a practical matter only in those cases where the student presents positive evidence of ill will or bad motive" (*Gasper*, 1975, at 851). A federal judge in Iowa succinctly underscored this concept when he declared that "The absence of such evidence coupled with the authorities' discretion to determine scholastic grades requires the decision in favor of defendants" (*Greenhill*, 1975, at 635).

In a landmark 1978 decision, *Board of Curators of the University of Missouri* v. *Horowitz*, the U.S. Supreme Court commented in great detail on the different standards to be used in disciplinary and academic cases. Charlotte Horowitz had challenged her dismissal from medical school on every imaginable ground, including of her human and constitutional rights (both procedural and substantive) and breach of what she claimed were certain standards that the school used in making academic and disciplinary decisions. A full discussion of the court's response can be found in Chapter Two. The court did not uphold her claim.

In *Giles* v. *Howard University* (1977), in which a student argued that the university should be held to the medical school retention policies in effect at the time of his matriculation, the U.S. district court found no violation of the student's rights. It was shown that the school had made reasonable changes in standards and that the university had gone out of its way to help the plaintiff remain in medical school without compromising its academic standards (*Giles*, 1977, at 606). The court made it clear that, since institutions reserve to themselves the right to dismiss a student who fails a course, it is apparent that they "also reserved the right to require such a student to comply with any reasonable condition to retain his student status" (*Giles*, 1977, at 606). Accordingly, the student's contract claim was denied.

Within the area of academic dismissals, courts have uniformly held that commercial contract doctrines should not be applied rigidly. Students must be prepared to read and understand the regulations affecting their continued academic good standing. In *Lyons* v. *Salve Regina College* (1977), the court cautioned the student that merely because a faculty panel made a "recommendation" in her favor, its use of that word did not preclude higher college authorities from making an adverse decision. Obviously, the First Circuit relied on the universally recognized chain of command at institutions of higher education.

From the court decisions just cited, it appears that, in the area of academic standards, use of a reservation of rights or a disclaimer can be helpful if the institution's decision is challenged. Courts seem to give even more leeway to faculty academic decisions than they do to disciplinary determinations, but the importance of a reservation or disclaimer cannot be overemphasized.

Changes in Requirements. Recently, the question of a university's right to alter or redefine course or graduation requirements has been litigated. The old *Niedermeyer* argument that the parties entered into a continuing and basically inalterable contract upon original matriculation has been all but obliterated by a series of cases beginning with *Mahavongsanan* v. *Hall* (1969). Georgia State University added to and changed graduation requirements after the student matriculated. The court held that the change in graduation requirements was "a reasonable academic regulation within the expertise of the University's faculty" (*Mahavongsanan*, 1969, 450). The court found that the student had received reasonable notification of the new graduation requirements and that the university had made efforts to devise a special program to resolve her dilemma. Finally, the Fifth Circuit rejected the breach of contract argument out of hand, stating: "Implicit in the student's contract with the University upon matriculation is the student's agreement to comply with the University's rules and regulations, which the University clearly is entitled to modify so as to properly exercise its educational responsibility" (*Mahavongsanan*, 1969, at 450).

Many jurisdictions have followed this rationale. Other important cases include *Hines* v. *Baker* (1981), *Craft* v. *Board of Trustees of the University of Illinois* (1981), *Anderson* v. *Banks* (1981), and *Lavash* v. *Kountze* (1979). The courts continue to defer to the necessary evolution of academic process and programs and to the expectations of both parties to the contract. Indeed, it can be argued that the average college student is not a total innocent. After twelve or more years of public or private education, the student should be sophisticated enough to realize that discretion is built into the educator's or administrator's role. Where it can be shown that the institution has exercised its judgment without malice or discriminatory intent or result, the student who challenges an academic failure or dismissal or a change in academic criteria will have no case.

Quality of Academic Programs. Claims based on contractual law in the area of quality or adequacy of academic programs have also increased. One of the first cases was *Ianiello* v. *University of Bridgeport* (1977), in which the student claimed that the institution was in breach of contract because the course content and what the student gained from the course were not consistent with the contractual promises contained in the course catalogue. The Connecticut trial court refused to allow the issue to go to a jury because the plaintiff had failed to sustain her burden of proof. However, it was clear that, if the plaintiff had produced appropriate expert testimony to counter the educational experts presented by the institution, her case would have gone to the jury.

Courts have imposed very strict standards on schools when the quality or availability of a certain program has been altered. In *Behrand* v. *State* (1977), the student catalogue had indicated that the school of architecture at Ohio University was fully accredited. During the plaintiff's attendance, the academic program deteriorated, and the school lost its accreditation; for this reason, Behrand held the university accountable in breach of contract. The plaintiff had relied on catalogue descriptions and matriculated with the intention of graduating from an accredited program. This reliance, and especially the payment of significant tuition monies, created the contract.

In *Peretti* v. *State of Montana* (1979), students whose course of study was interrupted by a cut in legislative appropriations argued successfully that they had the contractual right to complete the training period of six academic quarters and to receive a diploma evidencing such completion. The state was held liable to each of the numerous student plaintiffs. The Federal appellate court limited its reversal of the case to Eleventh Amendment grounds of governmental immunity and declared that no money could be awarded out of state coffers. *Peretti* continues to be widely and favorably cited for its contract arguments.

In *Lowenthal* v. *Vanderbilt University* (1977), the court ordered substantial damages to students in the doctoral program at the graduate school of management as a result of significant changes in the course of study. The court adopted an ends-oriented test. It acknowledged that a rule change alone is not enough to constitute a breach of contract, but it also found that the changes in the program were so severe that the doctoral program had, in essence, ceased to exist as a matter of fact. The court recognized that, at least in this case, the contract between the parties was one of "adhesion." Courts often refuse to enforce contracts that are exceesively one-sided and in which the relative bargaining positions of the parties are unfairly unbalanced. In *Lowenthal,* the court found that Vanderbilt received substantial tuition and gave little or nothing in return.

Cases of this nature present a problem for schools that also face financial straits or decreased enrollment. To avoid all possibility of litigation, an institution would have to include in the catalogue a disclaimer stating that the viability of each and every academic program was subject to periodic review, loss of accreditation, or cancellation at the sole discretion of the school at any time. Of course, such a disclaimer policy would make it difficult for the admissions office to attract applicants.

Lest anyone think that it is only the written representation that presents dangers, it should be noted that, in *Healy* v. *Larsson* (1971), a New York court held that, where a college official laid out an academic program and told the student that successful completion of this program would lead to award of a degree, the student was entitled to the degree, notwithstanding the facts that the program was insufficient and that it did not satisfy normal school requirements. There is no doubt that a college official can make statements that contractually bind the institution. This official (or other school employee) must have the apparent authority to make the representation or statement; absent this type of authority, the institution is not bound. The higher the person stands in the academic or institutional chain of command, the more reliance can be placed on the statements or promises. While it would be absurb to claim that the statements of an instructor were the official policy of the institution, every person has a level of responsibility that a reasonable student can rely on to credit the statement; the institution would thus be bound.

Refunds. Most catalogues describe a tuition refund policy—usually a proration of billed or paid fees, depending on the date of withdrawal. Institutions argue that, by accepting a student, they are committed to certain fixed expenses, especially for faculty salaries, which are based on enrollment, and that these fixed expenses continue, whether a particular student is present or not. It is always a question of fact—hence, it is always an issue to be determined at trial—whether a particular tuition refund plan is fair and equitable (*Cazenovia College* v. *Patterson*, 1974). An institution could choose to rely on the strict rules and regulations outlined in the catalogue, but a court, exercising its inherent, equitable power, could determine that an institution was unjustly enriching itself by strict enforcement of its refund policy. Again, the facts of the case would control.

To illustrate, at a school with a residence hall waiting list, a student's withdrawal from the residence hall would impose little if any financial hardship on the institution. To impose a significant penalty on the withdrawing student when the residence hall room would be immediately occupied at full rental by a new student is manifestly unfair. The school might be able to justify a small penalty to discourage disruption in the living arrangements at the residence hall and to cover administrative costs. In contrast, if the school had a number of empty beds, loss of one residence hall occupant could impose a significant financial hardship on the institution, absent a rigid refund policy.

In determining whether the refund policy—that is, the contract—should be strictly enforced against the student, most courts will seek to determine which party was responsible for breach of the contract. The student bears the burden of proving that the withdrawal was prompted by a material breach of the school's obligations. The concept of material breach of contract was recognized by a New York court in *Paynter* v. *New York University* (1971), where a student sought to hold the university liable for refund of tuition as a result of breach of contract when classes were cancelled after the Kent State incident. The New York court found that the closing was within the discretion of the institution; in light of such a minor breach, the court would not interfere with this discretion. In another case occasioned by the Kent State incident, a student failed to prove his claim that he was a third-party beneficiary of the contract between the instructor and the school. If his claim had been upheld, he would have been awarded damages based on the failure of his professor to teach in accordance with his employment contract (*Zumbrun* v. *University of Southern California*, 1972). Students who make contractual claims must not only surmount both the broad discretion traditionally given to school administrators and the judiciary's unwillingness to interfere but also prove that contract documents, such as the catalogue, do not specifically provide for such discretion.

The importance of an appropriate disclaimer is underlined by some recent cases involving changes in tuition during the student's academic career. The equitable principles of contract law recognize that it may be impossible for one party to perform a contract. While a court will not protect a party who has simply made a bad deal, the contract may be altered if the circumstances are beyond the party's control, especially if a disclaimer is part of the contract. Accordingly, even a school that optimistically projects moderate tuition increases but that later is forced to impose radical increases is protected. Among the leading cases in this area is *Basch* v. *George Washington University* (1977), where the court found that a general catalogue statement projecting future tuition was far too indefinite to create an enforceable promise, even though over a two-year period tuition rose from $3,200 to $12,500. The rationale of the *Basch* case was followed by an Illinois court in a case involving medical students at Northwestern University (*Eisele* v. *Ayers*, 1978). However, a Kansas trial court refused to give absolute discretion to the institution in tuition increases (*Hermann* v. *Hiersteiner*, 1978).

In short, courts increasingly are rejecting the theory of the *Niedermeyer* case that the initial contract of enrollment continues throughout the entire course of study. Instead, the courts have adopted what appears to be a more reasonable rule that the school has the right to make changes, with appropriate notice, from time to time in such areas as tuition. Courts will not force an institution to operate at a financial loss, which would adversely affect the quality of the education that the school could provide.

Student Discipline. *Dixon* v. *Alabama State Board of Education* (1961) made it clear that the general concept of procedural due process was appropriate and necessary in student discipline cases, at least in public institutions. Accordingly, most institutions have adopted disciplinary or conduct codes that set forth procedures to be used in the event of a problem requiring investigation, disciplinary action, or both. (See Chapter Two in this volume.) Most codes contain either a general or a specific list of offenses and possible sanctions, as well as detailed procedures for handling them. The wise institution recognizes that the student disciplinary process is clearly not criminal — which means that it does not require the specificity found in a criminal indictment or proceeding — and keeps the list of offenses fairly general so that it retains appropriate latitude.

The courts have been most understanding if an institution strays innocently from due process procedures, especially where there has been no real prejudice. As a general constitutional principle, the administrative process, administered by lay administrators acting in good faith, will be upheld even if there is some departure from due process (*Bishop* v. *Wood,* 1976). However, once the procedures are codified as part of catalogues or student handbooks, they become part of the contract between the institution and the student. In such cases, an institution can satisfy the somewhat amorphous requirements of constitutional due process but still be exposed to liability for breach of contractual due process.

Clearly, private institutions have a great deal more latitude than publicly supported schools in defining standards of student behavior, possible sanctions, and procedures. However, private institutions can also be charged with breach of contract if they do not follow their own published procedures. Since the concept of state or federal constitutional due process applies to state-supported institutions, students at private schools can rarely if ever prevail on these grounds. They must rely solely on contract arguments to secure what can be called *appropriate process* rather than *due process.* In *Tedeschi* v. *Wagner College* (1980), the court expressed reservations regarding the strict applicability of the contract relationship; nevertheless, the court held that the school had to follow its own procedures. Federal courts also have expressed reservations about the application of strict commercial contract principles to the relationship between a student and an institution (*Slaughter* v. *Brigham Young University,* 1975). In any case, institutions are bound to follow their own published procedures.

Housing Contracts. At the time of this writing, no decisions involving the housing or dormitory agreement or the meals contract between students and institutions have been reported. There is no doubt that a court would apply contract principles to the interpretation of such an agreement. For that reason, institutions should review this document carefully to make sure that its language is appropriate; such documents should include disclaimers and reservations of rights.

For instance, the institution may want to consider whether the dormitory contract should contain some language on conduct and on the handling of unacceptable or disruptive dormitory conduct. Should such misconduct be placed under the general student conduct or disciplinary code, or should there be special provisions and procedures pursuant to the dormitory contract itself? Should there be clauses allowing the institution to transfer the student for general reasons, such as the best interests of the institution? Should the institution include language providing for immediate eviction in the event of a breach of dormitory rules and regulations in the contract itself?

Where dormitory occupancy is required, the dormitory contract may be interpreted as one of adhesion, and the court might review the respective bargaining positions of the parties when deciding whether a contract should be enforced. A student who must live in a campus residence hall has no bargaining position and must sign the contract regardless of the fairness of its provisions. Further, some schools are so located that adequate or comparable housing is not available within a reasonable distance. There, too, a student must sign a contract simply because other suitable accommodations are not available. For these reasons, the institution would do well to review its housing or meal contracts with an eye on the realities of the local real estate and restaurant markets. To the extent that the school's facilities are the only suitable accommodations that are readily available or that use of them is required by school policy, a student may be able to argue successfully that onerous contractual provisions should not be enforced.

The question can also arise as to what type of contract is involved. Both leases and licenses are contracts, but each involves potentially different rights and obligations. All states have procedures for terminating a lease and evicting a tenant. These procedures are usually cumbersome, expensive, and time-consuming. Accordingly, some institutions, like the University of Maine, place a statement in their residence hall agreement stating that the contract constitutes a license, not a lease. That statement has not been tested in a court of law, but its inclusion will allow the institution to argue that a contract can be terminated via simple legal procedures. The prudent institution will explore the laws and procedures of its particular jurisdiction to determine whether a dormitory contract is likely to be construed as a lease or as a simple license, and it will analyze the consequences that follow from each construction.

Other Cases. Some theories of recovery seem to defy categorization. For instance, a parent chooses a school because, among other things, it features strict dormitory parietal rules. Sometime during the enrollment period, the rules are liberalized, and the enraged parent sues the college. Faced with that fact pattern, a New York court gave great deference to the professional judgments of administrators and held that the rule change did not constitute a breach in the contract of admissions or enrollment (*Jones* v. *Vassar College*, 1969).

In a case that seems to have some interesting implications for schools with both an active intercollegiate athletic program and a substantial grants-

in-aid program (*Taylor* v. *Wake Forest University*, 1972), a student athlete sued
the university for continuation of his scholarship after he opted not to continue
his athletic career. While his grades were more than adequate and he had not
suffered any debilitating injury, the court held that his relationship with Wake
Forest was contractual — that is, that he had agreed to participate in intercollegiate athletics, in return for which he would be given a scholarship. The
court ruled that he had breached his contract and declined to enforce his
scholarship.

Recently, the national newswires publicized the decision of a workers'
compensation commission in a midwestern state that awarded benefits to an
injured college football player. The student successfully argued that his relationship with the institution was one of employer-employee, at least when it
came to football. Only time will tell whether this case is an isolated incident or
the beginning of similar claims throughout the country.

Required Information. Although discussion continues in Washington,
the federal government has not generally entered into the arena of controlling
university or college catalogues. One of the few exceptions is the requirement
that institutions make certain consumer-type information available, especially
for recipients of financial aid. These regulations, contained in part 178 of Title
45 of the *Code of Federal Regulations*, have been in effect since November 18,
1977. It is significant that the regulations require only that consumer-oriented
data (such as scholarship or grant criteria, total cost of attending the institution, refund policies, student retention, and so forth) must be available on
request, not that they must be contained in a formal catalogue or made generally available to students. At least one state, New York, now requires such
data to be included in the catalogue or otherwise made available to all students. Student affairs administrators need to monitor moves to establish such
legislation in other states.

Disclosures of information or the creation of certain procedures can
also be required by federal programs controlling veteran's benefits, Title IX,
Section 504 of the Rehabilitation Act of 1973, the Family Educational Rights
and Privacy Act of 1974, and the like. The Federal Interagency Committee on
Education pamphlet *Keeping Your School or College Catalog in Compliance with Federal Laws and Regulations* provides helpful guidance.

The Role of the Student Affairs Administrator

Part of the responsibility of the student affairs administrator is to limit,
or at least to control, potential institutional contractual liability. Here are
some guidelines for administrative action that can serve as a useful starting
point:

- Consider a periodic and careful review of all printed material, including admission brochures, catalogues, student handbooks,
  syllabi, and the like. Times do change, and claims made yesterday
  are not always valid today.

- Include appropriate disclaimers in this material. Make sure that requirements or policies are not so specific as to preclude the reasonable exercise of good faith discretion. This holds true for academic as well as for athletic and disciplinary matters.
- Clarify the academic or administrative level at which final discretion will be exercised in both internal policies and published materials.
- Make sure that all professional employees understand that anything they say or write can be considered a contractual representation of the institution and that it is therefore potentially binding.
- In administering the affairs of the institution, act in good faith. Courts are loathe to interfere with the good faith decision-making process in higher education.
- Do not be afraid to request assistance of legal counsel, even in the earliest stages of a challenge based on a so-called contract.
- Never apologize for making a difficult decision or ruling. An apology can be taken as a sign of weakness and actually encourage litigation.
- Be sensitive to the fact that a potential litigant will often go from office to office seeking a sympathetic ear, support, or a slip of the tongue. Insist that the student follow the proper administrative chain of command on any specific policy that has been promulgated to deal with the particular situation.

These guidelines can help to avoid contractual litigation. Legal challenges to institutions of higher education are growing in the area of contract law. The prudent administrator should be aware of contractual representations and attempt to avoid unrealistic or unenforceable legal contracts.

References

Bender, L. W. "Will Your Catalog Stand FTC Scrutiny?" *American Governing Board Reports,* March/April 1976, pp. 1–3.
Federal Interagency Committee on Education. *Keeping Your School or College Catalog in Compliance with Federal Laws and Regulations.* Washington, D.C.: U.S. Government Printing Office, 1979.

George M. Shur, a partner in the Portland, Maine, law firm of Bernstein, Shur, Sawyer, and Nelson, specializes in the law of higher education. Coauthor of "Legal Liability of Faculty" in Legal Issues for Postsecondary Education *(American Association of Community and Junior Colleges, 1975), he has lectured extensively.*

Requests by individuals and groups to have access to and use the
facilities of public colleges and universities are increasing.
Under what conditions must an institution open its doors
to nonaffiliated individuals?

Facility Use Policies: Reducing Litigation Risks

Margaret J. Barr

The governor of the state wishes to hold a political fund raiser in the student center ballroom. The local heart association wants to hold a national convention on university property. A company asks for free space in the residence halls to sell products to students at a substantial discount. A religious group wants to rent the football stadium for a healing service. The local Kiwanis chapter asks permission to hold meetings each week in the student center. An antinuclear group seeks to distribute literature in the hallways of classroom buildings. Such requests for use of university facilities are not unusual. In fact, most student affairs administrators must decide on the legitimacy of such requests every week. The response of the administrator is crucial, for precedents can be set, and unlawful refusal can cause expensive and time-consuming litigation.

This chapter is designed to provide guidelines that enable student affairs administrators to respond to such requests. The focus is on public colleges and universities, both because they are more apt than their private counterparts to receive such requests and because there are many more legal constraints on their action than there are on the actions of their private counterparts. Development of sound facility use policies is essential for both the public and private sector; therefore, the guidelines presented here should also be examined carefully by administrators in private institutions.

M. J. Barr (Ed.). *Student Affairs and the Law.* New Directions for
Student Services, no. 22. San Francisco: Jossey-Bass, June 1983.

During the last two decades, many public colleges and universities have expanded their facilities, constructing arenas, auditoriums, stadiums, student centers, and recreation buildings. Such facilities are attractive and suitable for large public gatherings or meetings by groups or individuals not directly connected with the institution. Often, the meeting rooms and special use facilities are the best or the only facilities of their kind in the local community. Requests for use of such facilities are growing. Each institution must develop policies that provide direction to administrators faced with requests for facility use. Simply stated, a sound facility use policy needs to define how such facilities are to be used, by whom, and under what conditions.

Policy development can be relatively easy when it concerns internal matters or internal constituency groups. The questions become more complex when guidance is needed on the appropriate use of institutional facilities by individuals, groups, and organizations not directly affiliated with the institution. Such policies must be consistent not only with the purpose and mission of the institution but with the law. The sources of legal constraints on facility use policies involve constitutions, statutes, and judicial decisions. Each source will be discussed in detail in this chapter.

Constitutional Constraints

Nonaffiliated individuals and groups have five constitutionally protected rights, which must be taken into account in the development of facility use policies: freedom of religion, freedom of the press, freedom of speech, equal protection under the law, and due process.

Freedom of Religion. The principle of separation of church and state has long been used as a basis for denying permission to religious organizations to use public educational facilities. Complete exclusion of religious groups, however, may neither be prudent nor legally defensible, as court cases illustrate.

The First Amendment of the United States Constitution provides that Congress may make "no law respecting an establishment of religion or prohibiting the free exercise thereof" (U.S. CONST. amend. I). The United States Supreme Court has established guidelines to determine when the principle of separation of church and state has been violated or when the action taken by the state has interfered with the free exercise of religion.

In *Lemon* v. *Kurtzman* (1971), the Supreme Court held that acts of the state must have a secular legislative purpose (*Lemon*, 1971, at 2112) and that there may not be excessive governmental entanglement with religion. In *Hunt* v. *McNair* (1973), the Court held that the primary effect of an act by the state may be neither to aid nor to inhibit religion. The right of free expression of religious beliefs in a public park was upheld by the Supreme Court in *Fowler* v. *Rhode Island* (1953).

State courts faced with cases involving use by religious groups of facilities of public colleges and universities have followed the same logic. In *Keegan* v. *University of Delaware* (1975), a state supreme court held that neutral accommodation of religion is permitted in the facilities of a state university. The university had denied the use of a room in a residence hall for a religious service, arguing that public funds could not be used to support religion. The court denied the university's claim, indicating that, while promotion and advancement of religion is not permissible, the state must show a compelling state interest to deny the free exercise of religion. Moreover, religious groups must conform with facility use policies applicable to other organizations.

In Arizona, the board of regents rented the university stadium to Billy Graham, and a taxpayer brought suit, charging that the principle of separation of church and state had been violated (*Pratt* v. *Arizona Board of Regents*, 1974). According to this court, rental of the stadium to a religious organization did not violate the constitutional principle of separation of church and state, as long as fair rental value was charged for use and the use was of an occasional nature. The court did indicate, however, that "lease to a religious group on a permanent basis would be entirely different, because by permanancy the prestige of the state would be placed on a particular religion" (*Pratt*, SUPRA, 1974, at 517).

Finally, in *International Society for Krishna Consciousness of Atlanta et al* v. *Eaves* (1979), the Fifth Circuit declared two principles bearing on the separation of church and state doctrine. These principles have implications for higher education facility use policies, although the case in question involved distribution of literature and solicitation of funds at a city-owned airport. First, vague measures regarding such activity permit low-level administrative officials to act as censors; such measures cannot be permitted. Second, for a city to treat exchanges of money for commercial purposes differently from exchanges of money for religious purposes amounts to discrimination on the basis of content; therefore, such discrimination is invalid.

Freedom of the Press. *Marsh* v. *Alabama* (1946) is often cited as precedent in determining the right of colleges and universities to regulate the sale or distribution of off-campus publications on campus property. Although *Marsh* concerned the distribution of religious material on the public streets of a company-owned town in Alabama, the findings of the court are important in cases involving freedom of the press. The court held that "Neither a state nor a municipality can completely bar the distribution of literature on its streets, sidewalks, or public places or make the right to distribute dependent on a flat license tax or permit to be issued by an official who could deny it at will" (*Marsh*, 1946, at 277).

Texas Tech University banned the sale and distribution of one issue of a periodical newspaper on campus and based the denial on the grounds that the issue contained lewd or obscene language, and the university was taken to court (*Channing Club* v. *Board of Regents of Texas Tech University*, 1970). Citing the *Tinker* standard and indicating that the university did not prove that distribution of the issue constituted a clear-cut and present danger to the institution, the court held that the university had no valid reason to interfere either with content or with manner of expression.

When the Board of Regents of the University of Texas System sought to stop distribution of an underground newspaper on the Austin campus, it was challenged by litigation (*New Left Education Project* v. *Board of Regents of the University of Texas System*, 1970). Board of regents rules did not permit distribution of any off-campus newspaper without specific permission. After protracted court proceedings, during which the regental rules in question were repealed, the court held that the original rules were "unconstitutionally vague and also invalid leasing arrangements affecting First Amendment rights without adequate guidelines" (*New Left*, 1970, at 158). The amended regulations define solicitation, designate specific authority to authorize solicitation, and specifically exempt vending machines from the solicitation regulations.

In Arizona, the state supreme court used similar logic when the university was challenged in regulations that restricted the distribution of off-campus newspapers on campus property (*New Times, Inc.* v. *Arizona Board of Regents*, 1974). The university required a permit, payment of a fee, and registration of the newspaper with campus authorities, and it restricted distribution to vending machines. These regulations were held to be unconstitutional. The court indicated that access to the property for the exercise of First Amendment rights can be restricted when such property is not ordinarily open to the public. In the case at hand, however, the court held that "The state has already opened the campus to the public generally and may not arbitrarily restrict the freedom of individuals lawfully on the campus to exercise their first amendment rights" (*New Times*, 1974, at 173).

In a recent case in Illinois, a federal district court judge issued a preliminary injunction against enforcement of a college policy that prohibited the sale of literature in the student center (*Spartacus Youth League* v. *Board of Trustees of Illinois Industrial University*, 1980). Nonstudents distributed and sold political literature in the student center lobby. After repeatedly being warned to stop, the nonstudents were arrested and charged with criminal trespass. During protracted court proceedings, the university amended the challenged regulations, although nonuniversity persons still had to comply with identification and permission requirements also used with student organizations. The nonstudents amended their complaint, alleging that the student center and the outdoor public walkways on campus were public forums. The judge granted the injunction, holding that the student center and the campus walkways were public forums and that nonstudents have constitutionally protected rights in such public areas. This case raises serious questions with regard to the parts of institutional property that can be declared public and thus not subject to stringent regulation.

Freedom of Speech. Many cases have been tried regarding the use of university facilities to exercise First Amendment rights to freedom of speech. Administrators are constantly faced with the dilemma of balancing students' rights of free speech with the right of the institution to carry out the process of education free from outside interference.

Early cases dealt only with outside speakers, but they have had a great influence on public access questions. In a case involving Auburn University, the court held that Auburn could "establish neutral priorities and require adequate coordination" but "that it cannot altogether close its available facilities to outside speakers" (*Brooks* v. *Auburn University*, 1969, at 198). In *Stacey* v. *Williams* (1969), the district court held that, once a university "opens its lecture halls, it must do so nondiscriminately" (*Stacey*, 1969, at 971). "The facilities of state colleges and universities dedicated as they are to the specialized function of education may be used solely for that purpose" (Annoted 5 *American Law Review Federal 3d,* at 855). If any outside speakers are permitted, then speakers cannot be barred solely on the basis of the content of their speech. Freedom of expression has been protected by the courts, within the bounds of obscenity and incitement to action.

Restrictions on the use of campus facilities have been upheld in the courts as long as the restrictions are enforced in a fair and equitable manner (*Cholmakjian* v. *Board of Trustees, Michigan State University,* 1970). However, in *American Civil Liberties Union of Virginia* v. *Radford College* (1970), the court said, "While it might be constitutional to deny use of its facilities to all outside speakers, it is clearly unconstitutional to allow some outside speakers to use the facilities but to deny their use to speakers who are controversial or considered undesirable by the College administration, Board of Trustees, or State Legislature" (*A.C.L.U. of Virginia,* 1970, at 895).

The prime educational purpose of the institution may be protected through facility use policies. In *State* v. *Jordan* (1972), the court held that, even if a university is considered a public institution subject to public use, faculty, students, and the general public may not use the university in a manner that prevents use by others or that subverts its prime educational purpose.

Certain forms of written expression, such as handbills, have also been viewed as protected speech. The court of appeals in Arizona indicated that a blanket prohibition of handbilling in areas generally open to the public was not permissible (*Jones* v. *Board of Regents of University of Arizona*, 1970).

The right of an institution to bar commercial sales and solicitation on university property has also been challenged in the courts. At the district court level, a university regulation limiting the conduct of a person selling cookware on campus was upheld as constitutional (*American Futures Systems, Inc.* v. *Pennsylvania State University*, 1979). The Third Circuit reversed that finding on appeal and remanded the case back to the district court after lengthy court proceedings (*American Futures System,* 1982). Although some have viewed the Third Circuit ruling as giving status to commercial speech under the First Amendment free speech doctrine, a careful reading of the opinion does not justify that broad conclusion. Citing *Central Hudson Gas and Electric Corp.* v. *Public Service Commission* (1980), the court summarized the constitutional test for restrictions on commercial speech as follows: To be protected, it must be lawful and not misleading, and there must be substantial government interest in the restriction. According to the court, the institutional regulation that restricted the content of demonstrations as opposed to the conduct of demonstrations did not indicate a substantial government interest. The court further indicated that the case was remanded because "The district court does not appear to have considered the students' associational and free speech rights in the activities in their dormitory rooms independently from the activities conducted in the common areas" (*American Futures Systems*, 1982, at 14). Without a doubt, litigation in the area of commercial free speech on university property will continue to be active.

Equal Protection. The federal Constitution provides that all citizens have equal protection under the law and that citizens may not be treated differently merely due to their particular status. The courts have applied two different tests to determine if actions by school authorities are in violation of the equal protection clause of the Fourteenth Amendment. When the traditional test is used, there must be a rational relationship between the action of the state and the classification created by the state (*Lau* v. *Nichols*, 1974). The strict judicial scrutiny test is used in equal protection cases if and only if the interest of the individual is fundamental and if the classification that is being created by state action is suspect (*Reed* v. *Reed*, 1971).

Application of the equal protection clause to educational institutions rests on the principle that, once the state undertakes to provide a service or opportunity for one individual or group, it must provide the service or opportunity for every individual or group. This principle has caused litigation under the equal protection clause when nonaffiliated groups or individuals have been denied use of school facilities. Because use of school facilities is not a fundamental interest, the traditional test has been used by the courts to reach decisions in this area.

In general, the courts have held that standards for the use of public institutional facilities must be formulated specifically and objectively (Emerson, 1963). *American Civil Liberties Union of Southern California* v. *Board of Education, City of San Diego* (1961) and *American Civil Liberties Union of Southern California* v. *Board of Education, City of Los Angeles* (1961) are public school cases that support this concept. Both school boards required those who wished to use school property to sign a statement saying that the property would not be used to advocate overthrow of the government by force or violence. In both cases, the regulation was declared unconstitutional. In both cases, the court held that such a requirement was prior restraint on freedom of speech and that it denied equal protection to potential users.

In another public school case that has implications for higher education, the court held that "The state is not under a duty to make school buildings available for public gatherings, but if it elects to do so, it must be done with reasonable nondiscrimination equally applicable to all and equally administered to all" (*East Meadows Community Concerts Association* v. *Board of Education*, 1966). Elimination of certain groups from consideration for facility use because of their beliefs has not been upheld by the courts.

Faculty and staff groups are also subject to the equal protection clause. When a university denied use of facilities to one union because it had a bargaining agreement with a rival union, litigation resulted (*Civil Service Employees Association, Inc.* v. *State University of New York at Stony Brook*, 1974). The court held that "The University has no obligation to make its facilities available to unaffiliated organizations, but if it does so, it is required by the Fourteenth Amendment and by articles one and eleven in the State Constitution to administer its regulations with equality for all" (*Civil Service Employees*, 1974, at 929). A similar conclusion was drawn in a case in Missouri, when the court found no compelling state interest in denial of use of the institution's mail service (*University of Missouri at Columbia NEA* v. *Dalton*, 1978).

Rental of an auditorium on a regular basis for a nominal fee during nonschool hours was judged by the court to be effective dedication of the auditorium for the exercise of First Amendment rights (*National Socialist White Peoples Party* v. *Ringers*, 1973). In this the political party was refused rental of the auditorium on the basis of its racist statements and philosophy. The court held that the use of facilities partially dedicated as a public forum for expression of diverse views does not amount to state espousal of those views.

Due Process. An earlier chapter discussed due process requirements for student discipline in detail. These same due process requirements must also be met by public institutions when promulgating facility use policies. The Colorado Supreme Court held that nonstudents could not be denied right of access without notice and an opportunity to be heard (*Watson* v. *Board of Regents of the University of Colorado*, 1973). In *Dunkel* v. *Elkins* (1971), the University of Maryland barred a nonstudent from campus under a statute that authorized complete exclusion from state campuses of outsiders who had no lawful business to be there or who were disrupting the institution. The district court found in this case that, while the statute was constitutional, an outsider has a constitutional right to a hearing in connection with the order to exclude him from campus.

Statutory Constraints

Statutes at the federal, state, and local levels must also be respected when developing and implementing facility use policies. Each state has a unique set of civil and criminal laws. For that reason, an institution should test statutory concerns outlined against the applicable set of state statutes.

Authority over Facilities. In Chapter One, the legal status of colleges and universities was discussed. Legal authority to govern facilities and their use can make a critical difference in the development of policies. An institution's authority to construct facilities and regulate their subsequent use has been challenged in the courts. The Curators of the University of Missouri were found to have explicit statutory and state constitutional authority to issue revenue bonds and construct parking facilities (*State* ex rel *Curators of the University of Missouri* v. *Neill*, 1966). In Texas, the explicit authority of the Board of Regents of the University of Texas System to erect buildings and decide on their use was confirmed in *Splawn* v. *Woodard* (1926).

The courts have also upheld the implied powers of a governing board including regulation of facility use. In Arizona, the court held that "the Board of Regents has not only those powers expressly delegated to it but also such powers as may be reasonably implied for purposes of effectuating its purposes" (*Arizona Board of Regents* v. *Harper*, 1972, at 455). An Illinois court ruled that "The Board of Trustees has, by the statutes creating the University, the power and authority to do everything necessary in the management, operating, and administration of the University, including powers in the furtherance of the corporate purposes" (*Turkovich* v. *Board of Trustees University of Illinois*, 1957, at 305).

However, the claim of inherent powers on the part of the governing board has not received clear judicial support. In Texas (*Morris* v. *Nowotny*, 1959) and in New York (*Schuyler* v. *State University of New York at Albany*, 1968), the claim of inherent powers to regulate conduct and use of facilities has been sustained. Several successful court cases have been based on the premise that the concept of inherent powers provides too much discretionary authority for action by the institution (*Lieberman* v. *Marshall*, 1970; *Esteban* v. *Central Missouri State College*, 1969; *Smith* v. *Ellington*, 1971).

The clear power and authority of the governing board to regulate facilities and their use is the basis for policy formation and implementation. To proceed without such authority invites litigation.

Liability Concerns

Facility use policies for institutions of higher education should be developed and implemented in a manner that reduced the potential for liability claims against the institution. This goal is difficult to achieve in most higher education settings because policies are not often subject to strict legal scrutiny, because the institution's implementation structure permits great intrainstitutional variability in policy application, and because authority for day-to-day operations is not always clearly defined (Aiken, 1976, p. 129). For public institutions, the problem is complicated by the pervasive view that administrators, as agents of the state, have governmental immunity from suit.

Governmental Immunity. Although the Eleventh Amendment of the United States Constitution is often cited as a defense against liability, it only provides immunity from suit in federal court cases and immunity from liability judgments that must be paid from state treasuries (Aiken, 1976, p. 131).

Further, the vulnerability of public institutions to liability claims is greatly increased by the Fourteenth Amendment of the United States Constitution. A legal distinction is made between institutional actions that are governmental acts and institutional actions that are proprietary functions. A Kansas court declared that "A governmental agency is engaged in a proprietary activity when it embarks on an enterprise which is commercial in character or is usually carried out by private individuals or is for the profit, benefit, or advantage of the governmental unit conducting the activity" (*Carroll* v. *Kittle*, 1969, at 23).

In Arizona, a person fell in a stadium and was injured due to a defective condition; the facility was leased to a nonaffiliated group. The court held that governmental immunity did not attach (*Sawaya* v. *Tucson High School District*, 1955). A Virginia court viewed a similar fact situation in an entirely different manner. There, a patron fell and was injured while attending a concert in a leased auditorium. The court held that, because the lease was statutorily permissible, it should be viewed as a governmental function; thus, immunity was granted (*Kellam* v. *School Board of Norfolk*, 1975).

Many states and the federal government have also provided some form of limited waiver of governmental immunity in tort liability cases. Under such limited waivers of immunity, claims of liability are judged on the interpretation of the duty of the institution or agency to the plaintiff. Officials in state institutions should understand the limits of the governmental immunity claim within their state.

Negligence. In determining whether a public university is liable in negligence suits, the courts have made distinctions concerning the legal relationships between an institution and its invitees, licensees, and trespassers. An invitee is a person who is on the property because "he has been invited either expressly or by implication by the owner or possessor of the property" (Flora, 1970, p. I-59). A number of courts have held that the institution owes the duty of ordinary and reasonable care with respect to the condition of the premises for invitees (*Brown* v. *Oakland*, 1942; *Leahy* v. *State*, 1944; *Sandoval* v. *Board of Regents*, 1965). A licensee is on the property for his own convenience but at the sufferance of the property owner (Flora, 1970, p. I-59). For licensees, the institution owes the duty of maintaining the property in a reasonably safe condition. However, if ordinary hazards exist and the licensee is injured, the institution has not been held to be liable (*Mortiboys* v. *St. Michaels College*, 1973). In *Scully* v. *State* (1953), a nonaffiliated person was injured on a stairway while attending an on-campus movie. The court held that the university was not negligent. However, if the institution knew of a dangerous condition but allowed persons to use the property and if injury then resulted, liability could ensure. Under conditions where a person assumes the risk of injury and injury occurs, courts have not upheld liability claims against institutions and their agents (*Rubtchinsky* v. *State University of New York*, 1965; *Dudley* v. *William Penn College*, 1974). These decisions are critical to institutions that lease facilities to nonaffiliated groups for public events or that allow nonaffiliated spectators to attend events on institutional property.

In general, the courts have held that, when school property is leased to nonschool organizations, the lessee accepts the conditions of the facility by accepting the lease agreement. Such agreements should be negotiated carefully in order to reduce the potential for liability claims for negligence.

Civil Rights Liability. Section 1983 of the Civil Rights Act provides for liability in cases involving constitutional rights. A recent Supreme Court decision held that a municipality could not assert good faith as a defense against civil rights liability (*Owen* v. *City of Independence, Missouri*, 1980). Two cases have provided a foundation for determination of the extent of personal liability of school officials under Section 1983. *Scheur* v. *Rhodes* (1974) and *Wood* v. *Strickland* (1975) both place limitations on immunity from suit for persons acting in a governmental capacity. In *Wood*, the court set both the subjective and objective tests. Two questions were asked: Did school officials act without malice? and Did they know or should they reasonably have known that their actions would violate a constitutionally protected right? "*Wood* and *Scheur* taken together make it clear that the immunity extended to state officals is in fact a defense—a defense on the merits of both state of mind and reasonableness of conduct ("Developments in the Law, . . . ," 1977, p. 473).

Discrimination. Other chapters in this volume discuss the applicable federal antidiscrimination statutes. Although most of the case law on these statutes involves suits against alleged discrimination brought by students and faculty, the statutes can be applied in facility use questions. The facility use policies of public institutions are state action; thus, neither on their face nor by implication can such policies discriminate against any protected class of beneficiaries under federal law. Priorities in the use of facilities can be set to meet legitimate educational needs, but they cannot be based on discriminatory criteria.

Title VI of the Civil Rights Act of 1965, Title IX of the Educational Amendments Act of 1972, and Section 504 of the Rehabilitation Act of 1973 are enforced primarily by the threat of cutoff of federal funds to institutions. The courts have held that Title VI and Section 504 authorize an individual to bring a private legal suit to seek redress for alleged discrimination (*Cort* v. *Ash*, 1975; *Lau* v. *Nichols*, 1974). Administrators should be aware that, when private litigation can be brought, the institution may be liable for award of reasonable attorney fees to the prevailing party (Civil Rights Attorney's Fees Award Act of 1976).

Antitrust Laws. The courts have held in the past the the Sherman Act and the Clayton Act do not apply to postsecondary institutions when such institutions are engaged in governmental activities (*Parker* v. *Brown*, 1943; *Saenz* v. *University Interscholastic League*, 1976). However, in 1975 the Supreme Court declared that absolute exemption from antitrust coverage does not exist (*Goldberg* v. *Virginia State Bar*, 1975). As institutions attempt to generate additional income by leasing facilities for commercial and proprietary enterprises, their officers must be aware of the potential for litigation under the claim of restraint of trade. Care should be taken to assure that rental fees or charges are fair and equitable and that institutions do not combine with other educational institutions in the community to engage in price fixing on the cost of admission to such events.

The civil code of each state has other statutes that can influence facility use policies. Such statutes include statutes relating to general public safety, abuse of public office, public order and decency, weapon control, and police authority. Usually, public institutions are also subject to the general provisions of the state education code and the state election code. All these statutes must be considered in policy development.

Unfair Competition. There has been a long history of litigation between public colleges and universities and the local business community on the claim of unfair competition. The rationale on which such cases are based is the legitimacy of using state tax-supported property to conduct business activities that compete directly with private enterprise. Court decisions in such cases have been based on several factors, including the legal authority of the institution to engage in such enterprise, the nature of the goods and services rendered, and the rationale for the institution to engage in the enterprise. In *Villyard* et al. v. *Regents of the University System of Georgia* (1948), the court held that enterprises "reasonably related to the education, welfare, and health of student bodies" (*Villyard*, 1948, at 316) do not constitute unfair competition. In another case, the court held that a university may provide services to those not directly affiliated with the institution if it has the statutory authority to do so (*University of North Carolina* v. *Town of Carrboro*, 1972).

Relationships with Local Governments. A distinction is made between governmental functions and proprietary functions in determining the superiority of the state institution over local ordinances regarding general health and safety. In California, a university was not permitted to lease facilities to a circus under conditions that were not allowed under local ordinance (*Board of Trustees* v. *City of Los Angeles*, 1975). However, when the city of Boulder, Colorado, asked the court to compel the university to pay taxes on admissions to public events, such as concerts, lectures, and plays, the court declined to do so. As the state Supreme Court said, "The educational process is not merely for the enrolled students of the university but is part of the educational process for those members of the public attending events. A person's acquisition of knowledge should not be taxed" (*City of Boulder* v. *Regents University of Colorado*, 1972, at 123). The university did have to pay taxes on admission to athletic events.

Even under conditions of municipal home rule, it usually is only those activities at public institutions that clearly are not related to education that can be governed by local ordinances. The various units of local government are creatures of state policy, and they are subservient to the state in governmental functions, unless the state grants them authority to act (Fordham, 1975). Facility use policies, therefore, should conform to local ordinances when such policies govern activities that can legally be viewed as incidental enterprise.

Policy Guidelines

Public institutions of higher education are generally not legally obligated to make institutional facilities available for use by nonaffiliated persons. As a practical matter, however, total exclusion of all nonaffiliated persons from university property is difficult to achieve. Thus, for each institution, the issue becomes one of determining the conditions under which facilities can be used. Determination of such facility use policies is difficult, but it is necessary in order to protect the institution and to ensure fair and equitable use of public facilities. The following list of guidelines for development of facility use policy is based on the known legal constraints on such policies. As already indicated, however, the law is always evolving. The prudent administrator should not only assess the institution's current policies against these guidelines but also develop a process that allows regular policy review on the basis of informed legal advice.

- Facility use policies must conform to the general criminal and civil statutes of state and federal government.
- Facility use policies should be reasonably specific and precise on conditions for access to and use of campus facilities and property by nonaffiliated persons and groups.
- Facility use policies can regulate the time, place, and manner of use of institutional property by nonaffiliated persons and organizations.
- Facility use policies cannot discriminate on the basis of the beliefs or philosophies of requesting organizations.
- Facility use policies should set very specific standards for use of facilities by nonaffiliated religious, political, and commercial groups.
- Policies governing the sale and distribution of off-campus publications should be specific and precise.
- Facility use policies should stipulate the authority of the institution to refuse access under conditions in which there is strong evidence that such use of property will disrupt the educational enterprise.
- Facility use policies should stipulate due process standards, including procedures for appeal and review of decisions on facility use.
- All written policies should outline the management control prerogatives of institutional representatives.
- Facility use policies should specify the criteria to be used by institutional agents in policy implementation.
- Facility use policies should stipulate the individuals who have authority to make exceptions to policies.
- Facility use policies must address liability issues.

- Facility use policies should comply with antidiscrimination statutes.
- Facility use policies should define which areas of the campus, if any, are public areas, where free access and egress by nonaffiliated persons is permitted.

How to Begin

In order to achieve the minimal legal criteria set out in the preceding list, a number of procedural issues must receive attention in policy development. Awareness of these procedural issues can assist administrators involved in facility use policy development to develop policies that are not only consistent with identified legal constraints but that also reflect the unique needs of their institution.

Understand the Institutional Mission. Understanding the institution's educational and public service philosophy is the first step in development of a sound facility use policy. Indeed, this philosophic base is perhaps the most important factor in policy formation. To illustrate, a community-based institution and an institution committed to open access will both have parameters for facility use that differ from those of an institution with a restrictive environment. The institution's philosophy and mission define the parameters within which the legal constraints on facility use policies must be met.

Seek Legal Advice. While appropriate legal advice during the process of policy development does not guarantee that the resulting policy will withstand judicial scrutiny if it is challenged, it can assure that all identified legal standards have been included in the policy. Legal review has great potential for increasing the possibility that the final policy will be fundamentally fair and reasonable.

Raise Awareness. College and university administrators can no longer function in ignorance of the law. Every person who has policy formation responsibility needs to acquire at least a minimal understanding of the legal constraints on facility use policies. Acquisition of such understanding is a continuing process, because the law is ever changing. Thus, methods should be developed to assure that administrators are aware of new developments in the law. An informed person can provide better advice both when policy is being developed and when it is being revised.

Consolidate Policies. A consolidated policy for all institutional facilities provides the best defense against internal inconsistency. At most institutions, regulations on facility use can be found in handbooks, procedure manuals, and internal memoranda. If it is not feasible to develop a consolidated document, then, at the very minimum, a cross-reference index to all applicable policies is necessary in order to reduce confusion both for potential users of institutional facilities and for the institution's administrators.

Broaden the Policy Base. Policies need not only be legally correct, they must also be reasonable and useful to those charged with implementation. A

52

policy document provides guidance for everyday decisions. Inclusion of administrators who have responsibility for policy implementation in the policy development process has many advantages. Ambiguities can be resolved, potential problems can be identified, and clarity can be sought. An additional benefit is that a broad-based development process increases the knowledge base of all participants.

Summary

The development of legally sound facility use policies for public colleges and universities is not an easy task. Use of institutional facilities by non-affiliated persons or groups is a growing area of concern on most college campuses. Institutions of higher education are not immune from the law. Constitutional, statutory, and regulatory constraints can all affect the development of facility use policies. Institutions must therefore define the conditions under which nonaffiliated persons have access to and use of institutional property. Policies for the use of facilities must be fundamentally fair, clear, and concise, and they must provide adequate guidance for those charged with policy implementation. College and university administrators should anticipate problems with current policies, develop a sound procedure for revising policy, and assure that new policies meet identified legal standards. If they do, then the institution's own definition of the proper use of its facilities has a greater chance of surviving a test in the courts.

References

Aiken, R. J. "Legal Liabilities in Higher Education: Their Scope and Management." *The Journal of College and University Law,* 1976, *3,* 121–145.
Annoted 5 *American Law Review Federal 3d.* "Validity Under the Constitution of Regulation for Off-Campus Speakers at State Colleges and Universities," pp. 844–846.
"Developments in the Law, Section 1983 and Federalism." *Harvard Law Review,* 1977, *49,* 462–473.
Emerson, T. I. "Toward a General Theory of the First Amendment." *Yale Law Journal,* 1963, *72,* 877–956.
Flora, C. A. "Tort Liability and Insurance." In A. Knowles (Ed.), *Handbook of College and University Administration.* New York: McGraw-Hill, 1970.
Fordham, J. B. *Local Government Law: Legal and Related Materials.* Mineola, N.Y.: Foundation Press, 1975.

Margaret J. Barr is vice-president for student affairs at Northern Illinois University, DeKalb. This chapter is based in part on her unpublished doctoral dissertation, "Legal Constraints Governing Public Access to Facilities of Public Senior Colleges and Universities in the State of Texas" (University of Texas at Austin, 1980).

Student organizations exist at every college and university.
Student affairs administrators must be aware of the legal
responsibilities that attach to such organizations and
develop sound policies to minimize legal liability
in dealing with them.

Student Organizations: Some Legal Implications

Michael J. Cuyjet
Norden S. Gilbert
Patrick M. Conboy

Student organizations are a vital part of the extracurricular program at most colleges and universities. In the increasingly litigious society of today, however, student organizations are no more immune from legal concerns and the threat of litigation than the institution as a whole is. The courts have recognized that colleges and universities have certain obligations toward students who desire to associate with one another in an organized fashion for any number of purposes. The courts have also recognized that institutions have certain responsibilities relating to the operation of recognized student groups.

The nature of the relationship between university administration and campus student organizations can vary greatly from school to school. Generally, such a relationship has two major elements: formal recognition of the student organization by the institution and, within that framework of recognition, provisions allowing the organization to use services provided by the university. Such services usually center on use of university facilities for activities, an advisory relationship between the organization and individual faculty advisers or a central student activities staff, and access to institutional services. Institutional services can include access to university support areas, such as printing, postal service, physical plant maintenance workers, computer services, and accounting and budgeting offices; it can even include direct fiscal support from general university funds. Regardless of the intricacy of the relationship

M. J. Barr (Ed.). *Student Affairs and the Law.* New Directions for
Student Services, no. 22. San Francisco: Jossey-Bass, June 1983.

between an institution and its student organizations, responsibility and obligations rest on both parties. This chapter explores the legal obligations and the
institutional liability inherent in these obligations.

Recognition

The first issue of concern is the institution's obligation to recognize or
register student organizations. In this chapter, the term *recognition* is used to
mean the granting of official status by an institution to a group of students;
such status permits them to function on the campus and to use institutional
facilities in the pursuit of their extracurricular activities.

The Recognition Relationship. Recognition by the university is generally accomplished by one of three processes: automatic formal recognition,
selective formal recognition, and de facto recognition with no formal process.
The first process is the most prevalent. The institution establishes certain
criteria, which the student group must meet (for example, by submitting a list
of officers' names, addresses, and phone numbers and by securing a faculty
adviser). Any organization that meets these criteria obtains recognition.
Although this process seems fairly straightforward, litigation has occurred in
situations in which recognition criteria automatically eliminate certain groups
from recognition or in which conditional recognition restricts groups from full
use of university facilities. Prohibitions of recognition and restrictions on
facility use by student political and religious organizations have been tested in
the courts. In one recent case, *Widmar* v. *Vincent* (1981), the United States
Supreme Court rejected a ban by the University of Missouri Kansas City on
religious services by a registered student group. As part of its decision, however, the Court affirmed that the institution had the right and responsibility to
establish regulations on the allocation of space for extracurricular activities.

Selective formal recognition is similar to automatic formal recognition
because it, too, requires the student group seeking recognition to meet a
number of criteria. However, it differs from automatic recognition by requiring an official designate of the institution to review the group's application and
decide whether to approve it. The designate can be a single administrator, a
faculty or administrative committee, the staff of a university office (for example, the student activities office), or the institution's student government
body. Along with authority to grant recognition, the designate also has the
responsibility to see that the criteria are applied fairly and that there is no
opportunity for arbitrary and capricious action in the application of these
criteria.

Where recognition is de facto, a student group is recognized either
when it appears on a list published by the institution or when it uses university
facilities. Such a system holds considerable danger for an institution, both in
its lack of control and in its absence of safeguards to ensure responsible behavior. yet, there is another side to this laissez-faire approach: The court's finding

in at least one case (*Mozart* v. *State,* 1981) argues that the less control exercised over student groups, the less liability an institution has for their actions.

Denial of Recognition. Freedom of association to further an individual's personal beliefs has been held by the courts to be a constitutionally guaranteed right. Although freedom of association is not explicitly protected by the First Amendment, it has been held to be implicit in the freedoms of speech, assembly, and petition (*Healy* v. *James*, 1972). One way in which students exercise such freedom is by forming and participating in campus organizations. Although the courts are generally cautious about interfering with the control that a college or university exercises over its students, faculty, and facilities, it is well established "that neither students nor teachers shed their constitutional rights to freedom of speech or expression at the schoolhouse gate" (*Tinker* v. *Des Moines Independent School District*, 1969). Recognition of student organizations must therefore be addressed in the light of constitutional protections.

A university generally may not prohibit students from forming and participating in organizations. In *Healy* v. *James* (1972), the United States Supreme Court considered the denial of recognition by Central Connecticut State College to a local chapter of Students for a Democratic Society. The college president based his decision on his belief that the organization's philosophy was antithetical to college policies of academic freedom and unfettered discourse and on his concern about the relationship between the local chapter and the national organization, which admitted to a philosophy of violence and disruption.

The consequences of nonrecognition in *Healy* were significant. The organization was deprived of a forum on campus for announcing its activities, it was precluded from using campus bulletin boards, and it was barred from holding meetings on campus. This last restriction was driven home when chapter members were prevented from meeting in the student union coffee shop to discuss further action after the organization had been denied recognition. The Court rejected the argument that the college had withheld only its stamp of approval. The indirect limitations arising from nonrecognition were viewed as being as significant direct affronts to the right of association. It is interesting to note that the court did not question the right of the institution to control its facilities in this way. Such control was assumed to be properly within its province. Use of facilities and other privileges can be limited to duly constituted university groups as long as the recognition process is constitutionally acceptable.

The Supreme Court did not hold that all student organizations have an absolute right to recognition. However, provided that an organization follows all reasonable steps laid down for recognition, the burden is on the university "to demonstrate the appropriateness of [its] action" (*Healy*, 1972, at 2348). The Court recognized that a delicate balance must be struck, especially on a college campus, between "the mutual interest of students, faculty members, and administrators in an environment free from disruptive interference with the

56

educational process" and the "equally significant interest of the widest latitude for free expression and debate consonant with the maintenance of order" (*Healy*, 1972, at 2341). The second interest is especially vital in an academic community (*Shelton* v. *Tucker*, 1960). As grounds for nonrecognition, the Court has recognized "advocacy 'directed to inciting or producing imminent lawless action. . . . likely to incite or produce such action'" (*Bradenburg* v. *Ohio*, 1969, at 1928), actions that "materially and substantially disrupt the work and discipline of the school" (*Tinker*, 1969, at 740), and refusal to "affirm in advance [a] willingness to adhere to reasonable campus" rules and regulations (*Healy*, 1972, at 2350–2352).

A series of cases has been brought by on-campus homosexual groups to enforce their right to recognition. The *Healy* case is instructive in dealing with such cases, since they turn on the issue of First Amendment rights. Admittedly, the life-style espoused by such groups could be as socially offensive and abhorrent to some individuals as the political views of Students for a Democratic Society were to others during the Vietnam War. In *Gay Alliance of Students* v. *Matthews* (1976), Virginia Commonwealth University was ordered to register the organization and to afford it all privileges normally enjoyed by registered student groups. The court of appeals rejected the university's argument that the First Amendment rights of the students had not been denied, since the university was only withholding its official seal of approval. The university conceded that nonrecognition hindered recruitment and that it denied the organization some services normally available to university groups. The court also rejected the university's argument that registration would imply that the university approved of the group's aims and objectives. The university had registered other political, social, and cultural organizations without implying approval or endorsement of them. The fact that registration could encourage students to join the organization was held to be in accord with the First Amendment protection of freedom of association. As in *Healy*, the court raised no question about the university's right to regulate student conduct. The court's decision rested squarely on the First Amendment. The Gay Alliance had been formed to discuss homosexuality and to counsel homosexuals. The university remained free to regulate sexual activity.

Similarly, a district court in Tennessee rejectedthe argument of Austin Peay State University that recognition of a student homosexual organization would imply approval, noting the contradiction inherent in recognizing religious, political, and activities groups in general (*Gay Rights* v. *Austin Peay State University*, 1979). The court also distinguished conduct from advocacy of the acceptability of conduct. In this case, there was conflicting testimony on the issue of whether recognition of homosexual organizations could increase the incidence of homosexuality. The court, however, rejected the potential harm of ideas and information as a basis for rejection. Even if recognition of the student group would increase homosexual activity and even though homosexual behavior violated state law, the university could not abridge students' free speech and association, although it was free to enforce Tennessee's sodomy laws as vigorously as it saw fit.

In yet another case (*Gay Lib* v. *University of Missouri*, 1977), there was expert medical testimony that formal recognition could encourage homosexuality and result in the commission of felonious acts of sodomy. Nevertheless, the court held that this testimony was "insufficient to justify a governmental prior restraint on the right of a group of students to associate" for the expressed purpose of providing a forum for discussion of homosexuality (*Gay Lib*, 1977, at 848). The likelihood of imminent lawless action was deemed insufficient to justify abridgment of students' First Amendment rights.

In *Gay Activists Alliance* v. *Board of Regents* (1981), the Oklahoma Supreme Court rejected the regents' in loco parentis assertion that it had "discretionary duty to act for the benefit of the health, welfare, morals, and education of the university students," holding that "the exercise of such duty . . . cannot be influenced by personal tastes or be in violation of constitutional rights." In light of First Amendment concerns, the court rejected the notion that the university had "a duty to ensure that the purposes of recognized organizations reflect public policy as it is established by prevailing university community standards" (*Gay Activists*, 1981, at 1118). The university could enforce reasonable regulations as to time, place, and manner of activities, as long as the regulations were not unduly burdensome and as long as they were imposed equally on all campus organizations.

These principles, first established in *Healy* and elaborated in the student homosexual organization cases just cited, have been applied to followers of Sun Myung Moon and to members of his Unification Church. In *Aman* v. *Handler* (1981), the University of New Hampshire attempted to defend its refusal to give official recognition to the Collegiate Association for Research Principles. Applying the standards first established in *Healy,* the court ruled that the university had failed to justify nonrecognition.

Unfortunately, most court cases regarding the recognition issue have been brought in response to nonrecognition. This does little to define the legal relationship that develops when a university grants recognition to a student organization. If recognition does not imply approval, as ascertained in *Gay Rights,* what is the nature of the relationship between the institution and the student organization that it recognizes? Development of policies in the absence of clear examples is fraught with difficulties. In case law, however, some general principles are apparent. A recognized student organization does not become an agent of the university unless its specific purpose includes such a relationship with the university's administration. If recognition implies nothing more than permission to use university facilities at no charge or for less than outside groups are charged, this relationship is one between two parties in a contractual arrangement. This contractual arrangement assigns responsibilities regarding the safe and proper use of facilities to both parties, but the relationship itself falls short of an in loco parentis relationship. If the state incorporates the student organization as a separate entity, then a contractual view of the relationship has even greater validity.

Use of University Resources

It is well established that recognition of student organizations is deeply entrenched in the rights of students established by the First Amendment. Inherent in recognition is the right to use campus facilities, to have access to campus publications, to qualify for student funds, and in general to operate freely on campus.

Facility Use. The court applied the First Amendment rights in *Gay Students Organization* v. *Bonner* (1974). In this case, the University of New Hampshire attempted to prevent or curtail certain social activities of the gay student organization. The court stated: "The ultimate issue at which inquiry must be directed is the effect which a regulation has on organizational and associational activity, not the isolated and for the most part irrelevant issue of recognition per se" (*Gay Students Organization,* 1974, 652). Viewing social events as playing an important role in individuals' efforts to associate to further common beliefs, the court held that prohibiting all social events constituted a substantial abridgment of associational rights, although this abridgment was indirect. While the court recognized that the state had the power to regulate the time, place, and manner of communicative conduct to further substantial governmental interests, it permitted the state to exercise that power only as broadly as necessary. Once the public forum had been opened to student groups, selective exclusion based on content alone was impermissible.

The line of reasoning reported here should not, however, suggest that the court ignored the very real power of the university to regulate conduct on campus. Citing *Brandenberg,* the court stated: "Not only may [the university] act to prevent criminal conduct by policies focused on real and established dangers, but it can proscribe advocacy of illegal activities falling short of conduct, or conduct in itself noncriminal, if such advocacy or conduct is directed at producing or is likely to incite similar lawless action" (*Gay Students Organization*, 1974, at 662). As the court held in *Healy*, the university can go even farther: The court recognized the university's interest in assuring the traditional academic atmosphere by allowing it to proscribe disruptive behavior.

Obviously, the courts have drawn a thin, and sometimes a fuzzy, line between what the university can legitimately regulate and what it cannot. For example, the Florida Supreme Court stated that, once a university opens its buildings to student groups, it may not restrict such use in violation of First Amendment freedoms, but it also upheld the right of Florida State University to deny use of facilities to Students for a Democratic Society. The court found that the student organization planned to disobey university rules and regulations with the intent of causing disruption and disturbance on campus. The court recognized the university's duty to maintain order and to protect the campus from disruption (*Lieberman* v. *Marshall, 1970).*

Despite the relatively narrow range of activities that may be proscribed, recognition does not give student organizations unbridled access to university resources for every legitimate exercise of First Amendment freedoms. Whereas the university may not abridge such freedoms, the courts have not required the university to take an active role in furthering those freedoms. For example, in *National Strike Information Center* v. *Brandeis University* (1970), a student organization demanded that Brandeis make its computer, typewriters, and other equipment available to the organization. The court ruled that the university had no such obligation to students, finding "that a student association has no more right to demand that these facilities be made available to it than to demand that the President make his secretary available or that he make campus maintenance trucks or other vehicular equipment available to service the purposes of a student group" (*National Strike Information Center,* 1970, at 931).

Use of Student Fees. The courts have also recognized the university's right to limit the uses to which student fee monies can be put, even when such expenditures might contribute to the exercise of First Amendment freedoms. The Maryland Public Interest Research Group (PIRG) sponsored investigations into the social problems of students and the general public. The University of Maryland assisted the organzation by granting credit to student participants and by providing office space. However, it prohibited the use of student fee dollars for litigation. The court stated: "There is not affirmative commandment upon the University to activate Maryland PIRG's exercise of First Amendment guarantees; the only commandment is not to infringe their enjoyment" (*Maryland Public Interest Research Group* v. *Elkins,* 1977, at 865).

The courts have held that colleges and universities, unless otherwise prohibited by law, have the authority to establish, collect, and allocate mandatory student fee funds (Tanner, 1978). When the president of San Jose State University was sued by the student association for withholding funds because of its failure to provide athletic grants-in-aid, the court upheld the president (*Associated Students, Etc.* v. *Trustees of California State Universities and Colleges,* 1976). Student body organizations in the California state university and college system are authorized and established by statute; therefore, the court held that the president did not act unreasonably and that "It follows that a state university or college president may reject a student body organization's budget or financial 'program' when he reasonably concludes that it is not in conformity with the policy of the campus" (*Associated Students,* 1976, at 604).

As the general economic climate becomes more restrictive, litigation about use of student fees may increase. Several questions seem moot. For what purposes, including the purposes of special-interest groups, should student fees be allocated? Can individuals determine that they do not want their portion of the aggregate student fees to support particular student organizations?

Resource Use Policies. One common theme in much of the litigation in this area is that there are no clear guidelines for responsible behavior by the members of student organizations and no clear policies that outline the parameters of university responsibilities. The message is clear: Institutions must develop guidelines and policies and make them part of their working procedures. The key interest here is preparedness. By taking time both to develop clear policies and to disseminate them to student organizations, institutions can avoid most situations that might raise questions about unequal access.

The most important aspect of guidelines and policies is the principle of equal treatment for all student groups. For example, a well-designed, comprehensive policy for use of university classrooms by student organizations accomplishes a number of things: The policy is easy to publicize and distribute if it is in concise and readable written form. Individuals tend not to argue against or debate a policy that they feel is applied uniformly to all. Individual campus offices will apply such a policy uniformly. Finally, administrators do not have to make subjective decisions or to accept liability for the results of such decisions. It is precisely the situation in which an administrator has to interpret unclear guidelines on an ad hoc basis that is so perplexing. The problem is particularly serious where many different faculty or administrators serve as advisors to student groups. A faculty advisor's handbook is a sensible solution; on more and more campuses, it is becoming a necessary tool for avoiding accusations of unequal application of regulations.

A second important aspect of the application of policies on use of facilities is the practical question of enforcing compliance. Long and detailed regulations can be developed and printed. However, if the regulations are impossible to enforce uniformly or if they are difficult and time-consuming to police, all efforts to develop them may have been wasted. Furthermore, the student activities administrator's liability may actually increase if regulations cannot be enforced. Not only is the administrator unable to fulfill the obligation to oversee and police student activities, the administrator must often use the little existing enforcement power in an on-again/off-again manner, thereby openly inviting charges of subjectivity and unequal application of institutional policies. For the litigation-minded student who feels aggrieved, this could be an invitation to action.

Liability Issues

Once the issues of recognition and facility use have been addressed, the next major concern is that of the control that the institution exerts over the various activities of student organizations under its jurisdiction. There are two important questions: How much control can student activities administrators reasonably be expected to have over the individual actions of these organizations? And what constitutes negligence if such administrators fail to police the organizations' activities? In the current legal environment, the primary issue is not whether liability can attach but when it attaches to the institution and to the individual administrator.

Negligence. In a 1981 Court of Claims of New York case, the issue at

suit was the liability of the state of New York for publication of a libelous letter
in the student newspaper of the State University of New York at Binghampton
(*Mozart* v. *State,* 1981). Two students sued the state of New York for damages,
on grounds that the letter falsely stated that they were homosexual. The newspaper was supported by advertising and mandatory student activity fees. The
university assumed certain overhead costs, including office space. While students could earn independent study credit by working for the paper, the paper
was controlled and operated by the students themselves. The paper did not
have a faculty advisor, and the university had no policy guidelines regarding
the newspaper.

The court acknowledged two possible theories of liability: "(1) the
State, through the University, may be vicariously liable for the torts of the
[student newspaper] and its editor on the theory of *respondeat superior,* [that is],
the University, or principal, might be liable for the torts of its agents, the student paper and editors, and (2) the State, through the University, may have
been negligent in failing to provide guidelines to the newspaper staff regarding
libel generally, and specifically, regarding the need to review and verify letters
to the editor" (*Mozart,* 1981, at 603).

In deciding the case, the court held that the university — and, therefore,
that New York state — was not liable under the *respondeat superior* theory,
since neither the university nor the state had control over the conduct of the
student newspaper. Such control is necessary for a principal-and-agent relationship to exist. As to the negligence theory, the court found that it did not
apply in this case. The court was strongly influenced in its analysis by the fact
that, since it would have been unconstitutional for the university to exercise
prior restraint on the content of the newspaper, it could not have a duty to provide guidance to student editors in the matter of publication of libelous material. Since the institution was not in a breach of a duty, it could not be found
negligent. However, cases involving student newspapers are not entirely typi-
cal of the relationship between a student organization and an institution.
Thus, *Mozart* does not indicate how future courts may view the issue of institutional negligence in cases where the institution lacks policy guidelines for student organizations and their conduct.

Recently, the Ohio legislature considered a statute holding university
administrators responsible not only for improper student activities of which
they are aware but also for improper activities of which they reasonably should
have known. It will be very interesting to see whether the law passes. Subsequent court tests of the principle that administrators can be held liable for
actions of which they have no knowledge but of which they should have known
because of their administrative role should be carefully monitored.

Another case, *Bradshaw* v. *Rawlings* (1979), prompted a thorough discussion of the legal responsibility of Delaware Valley College for personal
injuries sustained by a student in an accident resulting from overconsumption
of alcohol at a class picnic. A jury decided that the college had been negligent,

and the court found on a posttrial motion by the college that the jury decision was reasonable. Bradshaw, who as a result of the accident had become a quadraplegic, had been in a vehicle driven by defendant Rawlings, whose alleged intoxication caused the accident. Rawlings became intoxicated at the class picnic. In permitting the jury decision to stand, the court relied on RESTATEMENT SECOND OF TORTS §§282, 283 (1965), which states: "Negligence is conduct which falls below the standard established by law for the protection of others against unreasonable risk of harm....The standard of conduct to which [one] must conform to avoid being negligent is that of a reasonable man under like circumstances."

One important consideration was that the sophomore class faculty advisor participated in the planning of the picnic and assisted in the disbursement of funds to purchase alcoholic beverages but neither attended the picnic nor sent a substitute. In addition, the college administration printed flyers notifying the sophomore class of the date and place of the picnic, and these flyers, which contained drawings of beer mugs, were displayed in prominent locations on the campus.

The decision of the district court denying the motion to set aside the jury decision was appealed in *Bradshaw* v. *Rawlings* (1979), and the United States Court of Appeals reversed the finding of liability against Delaware Valley College. The court held that times had changed and that beer consumption was common among college students. The court also pointed out "that the modern American college is not an insurer of the safety of its students. Whatever may have been its responsibility in an earlier era, the authoritarian role of today's college administrators has been notably diluted in recent decades. Trustees, administrators, and faculties have been required to yield to the expanding rights and privileges of their students....Today students vigorously claim the right to define and regulate their own lives" (*Bradshaw,* 1979, at 139). Because the institution had no specific duty to control and direct such events as a class party, it had no liability. However, in an earlier decision, the court held that an educational institution may be held liable for negligence in the supervision of extracurricular activities. In a high school case involving injury at an unsupervised initiation ceremony, the faculty advisor was found to be liable (*Chappel* v. *Franklin Pierce School District No. 402,* 1967).

While *Baldwin* v. *Zoradi* (1981) does not deal specifically with a student group, it is instructive on the issue of what duty is owed by an institution. In *Baldwin,* an individual seriously injured in an alcohol-related incident brought suit against the trustees of the institution and two resident assistants. The plaintiff's claim hinged on the fact that the student resident assistants knowingly permitted the consumption of alcohol in the residence hall, in direct violation of institutional regulations. Allowing the violation to exist contributed to the accident. For such an action to be upheld in California, there needed to be a special relationship between the plaintiff and the university. The court found that the residence hall license agreement did not constitute the required special relationship. Further, the court held that, even if there had been such a special relationship, the harm must be foreseeable. Further, the risk of harm must be "sufficiently high and the amount of activity needed to protect against harm sufficiently low to bring the duty into existence" (*Baldwin,* 1981, at 816).

The precise parameters of an institution's liability for actions of student organizations have not been defined clearly by the courts. At best, conclusions can be drawn by analogy from *Bradshaw, Baldwin,* and *Mozart.* A very realistic approach needs to be taken in determining if a duty exists. If the logic applied in *Bradshaw* is consistently followed in future cases, then liability will not be attached to institutions for negligent acts by student organizations, at least in alcohol-related cases. Further, *Mozart* seems to highlight some of the basic tests that courts seem likely to use in future analyzing whether an institution is liable for acts by student organizations. Under some circumstances, it seems, as the guidance and contact extended by the institution over student organizations diminishes, so also does its liability for their acts. However, if there is a special relationship between the student and the institution or if there is active negligence, liability will attach.

Student Civil Rights. The rights of students to assemble in groups and to exercise the rights and privileges granted to them by the institution have already been discussed. Although student activities administrators work primarily with students in organizations, they would be remiss not to consider the consequences of actions that violate the personal rights of individual students. While the decision handed down by the United States Supreme Court in *Wood* v. *Strickland* (1975) is not specifically related to the student activities area, it is still of great importance. This case was instigated by two students who had been expelled. The students brought suit for damages and other relief under Section 1983 of the Civil Rights Act. They claimed under the color of state law that their constitutional rights to due process had been violated. Faced with the fact that the lower courts were not in agreement about the nature of the immunity available to school administrators and school board members from awards of damages under Section 1983, the Court finally resolved the issue. The Court held "that (1) while on the basis of common law tradition and public policy, school officials are entitled to a qualified good faith immunity from liability for damages under the Civil Rights Act, they are not immune from such liability if they knew or reasonably should have known that the action they took within the sphere of official responsibility would violate the constitutional rights of the student affected, if they took the action with malicious intent to cause a deprivation of such rights or other injury to the student" (*Wood,* 1975, at 992). Furthermore, the Court stated that "the Civil Rights Act is not intended to be a vehicle for federal court correction of errors in the exercise of school officials' discretion that do not rise to the level of violation of specific constitutional guarantees" (*Wood,* 1975, at 994).

The Court was influenced greatly by public policy reasoning. It noted that, "although there have been differing emphasis and formulation of the common law immunity of public school officials in cases of student expulsion or suspension, state courts have generally recognized that such officers should be protected from tort liability under state law for all good faith, nonmalicious action taken to fulfill their official duties" (*Wood,* 1975, at 999).

The holding of the Court on the issue of compensatory damages does, however, limit the actual impact of personal liability. Compensatory damages were found to be appropriate only if a school official acted with impermissible motivation or with such disregard of the rights of students "that his action cannot reasonably be characterized as being in good faith" (*Wood,* 1975, at 994). In *Cary* v. *Piphus* (1978), the Supreme Court reduced some of the concern regarding compensatory damages under the Civil Rights Act. In *Cary,* the court ruled that the plaintiff had to prove that he had been injured by the deprivation of his rights before he could recover damages.

Prevention of liability actions and defense against such actions are complex and difficult for institutions of higher education. The problem is further compounded by their dealings with student organizations. Although it appears that reasonable good faith action under the facts and circumstances known at the time is the best guideline, education is needed. In this instance, ignorance is not bliss, and it will not be upheld in the courts.

Guidelines for Student Activity Administrators

The only sure thing about the legal implications of student activities is that there is no sure thing. Nonetheless, institutions can take some reasonable measures to assure safe, unfettered extracurricular activity by student groups on campus. First, the institution must define and develop clear, comprehensive policies on recognition of student organizations. Such policies must explain the responsibilities of all parties. They must stand the tests of equal application and noninfringement of basic rights guaranteed to students by federal, state, and local law. They must be disseminated across campus, so that all student organizations that may wish to use university facilities are aware of them and all university faculty and administrators who play a part in implementing such policies implement them uniformly. Such policies must also include a mechanism for periodic review and revision. The revision process should allow input from student organization representatives as well as from faculty and staff. "It will not suffice to merely adopt another institution's model of activity regulations. Each institution must formulate its own code of regulations and procedures" (Tanner, 1978, p. 68).

Second, the institution bears a responsibility for staff personnel who work with student organizations. In many cases, this responsibility extends to organization faculty advisors. It is incumbent on the institution to train student activities personnel and faculty advisors to enact the institution's policies on student organizations. Staff must be aware of university regulations and responsibilities. They must know the extent both of their authority and of their personal liability in the decisions that they make daily. As with policy development, this is an ongoing process. Not only must new staff be fully informed as part of their orientation, but current staff must be kept abreast of changes in policies as soon as they occur. Furthermore, staff development activities must also keep student activities staff attuned to the environment in which they must function. As situations within the environment change, so do factors affecting the operational relationship between student groups and the institution.

Third, the institution needs to develop a plan for its official response to litigation resulting from its relationships with student activities groups. It is far better to develop a procedure and hope it never has to be used than to face a potential lawsuit without a plan and have to develop one instantly. The plan will identify appropriate legal counsel both inside and outside the institution. It will assign specific roles to each of these persons as well as to other administrators who are involved. It will establish a chain of command among these individuals, delineating who is responsible for contacting others within the institution as the litigation ensues. It will also designate spokespersons, so that administrators understand clearly who speaks to the plaintiff or the plaintiff's representative, who informs the university community about the proceedings, and who speaks to the press on behalf of the institution. Once these roles have been established, strict adherence is vital to a successful effort.

The litigation response policy should also suggest the factors to be assessed in researching the situation under question. Basically, assessment is a plan for canvassing a wide range of university personnel who may have information of merit in preparing a legal response. However, assessment needs also to take a serious look at the political climate both on campus and in the surrounding community. Any major decision that affects an institution's direction must take campus and community politics into account (Barr and Keating, 1979). University involvement in litigation is no exception.

If the catch phrase of the 1960s was Peace and Love and of the 1970s, Do Your Own Thing, the phrase for the 1980s may prove to be See You In Court. Because student activities involve a vast number of people in myriad interpersonal relationships in an environment that prides itself on allowing more personal freedom than most other institutions in society, then an upswing in litigation involving student activities seems to be inevitable. Careful planning can help to lessen the negative impact of this phenomenon.

References

Barr, M. J., and Keating, L. A. (Eds.). *Establishing Effective Programs.* New Directions for Student Services, no. 7. San Francisco: Jossey-Bass, 1979.

Tanner, G. "Legal Aspects of Student Personnel Functions." In E. H. Hammond and R. H. Schaffer (Eds.), *The Legal Foundations of Student Personnel Services in Higher Education.* Washington, D. C.: APGA Press, 1978.

Michael J. Cuyjet is director of university programming and activities at Northern Illinois University; he has been a member of the board of directors of the National Association for Campus Activities.

Norden S. Gilbert is acting associate legal counsel and contracts administrator at Northern Illinois University.

Patrick M. Conboy is students' attorney at Northern Illinois University, where he created that office, which provides legal services to students in matters not related to university affairs.

University legal counsel can be an invaluable source of advice and help to the student affairs administrator at all stages of policy development and problem solving.

Use of Legal Counsel: Avoiding Problems

Shari Rhode

Society as a whole looks increasingly to the courts for resolution of its disputes. The university community is no different. Institutions of higher education have become complex operations that mandate an increased role for legal counsel in problem avoidance as well as in problem resolution. Campuses are faced daily with legal questions that range from personnel relationships to personal injuries, from entertainment negotiations to labor negotiations, from tax issues to general corporate issues and that include everything in between. As Markse and Vago (1980, p. 165) note, "Faculty and students, in particular, have turned to the law to protect individual rights and to check administrative discretion. . . . The era of collegiality is being replaced by one of liability. The heterogeneous, impersonal and, at times, almost alienated quality of the academic climate fosters the utilization of law to assert individual rights and to settle grievances in academic situations."

Since the issues that university administrators face today are so varied, competent legal counsel becomes more important than ever, not only to deal with the problems that arise but to provide information and opinions that permit administrators to make informed decisions. Legal counsel accomplishes the latter aim by delineating the legal ramifications of options being considered in the decision-making process. A treatise on the many roles of university legal counsel is well beyond the scope of this chapter. Thus, its purpose is to

M. J. Barr (Ed.). *Student Affairs and the Law.* New Directions for
Student Services, no. 22. San Francisco: Jossey-Bass, June 1983.

sensitize the reader to some of the ways in which day-to-day activities involve legal considerations and to ways in which university legal counsel can be used effectively.

No matter how overwhelming the complexities of the law seem to be, a student affairs administrator does not have to have a law degree in order to be good at the job. However, the student affairs administrator does need access to the services of a competent individual who understands the unique entity that is a college or university. This growing need has helped to create the professional specialty known as the university attorney. As Sensenbrenner (1974, pp. 13–14) observes, "The business today of a university of college ranges from one end to the other of any legal index one might select. On the other hand, though, this business takes place in an environment that is often baffling to the general practitioner. . . . Thus, one who works substantially or all of the time in the education law setting has all of the analogical advantages of being a generalist, while at the same time having a considerable advantage over adversaries not conditioned in the same environment."

Thus, competent legal counsel is an invaluable resource for the student affairs administrator. The question becomes one of maximizing the effectiveness of that resource. To do so, the administrator must understand the different roles that a university attorney can play. Every lawyer, whether working in house with an institution or in private practice, plays two general roles: advisor and advocate.

Legal Counsel as Advisor

The most important role in the overall scheme of higher education that legal counsel can play is the role of advisor. By assisting administrators in the process of developing policies that become the sources of rights and obligations for an institution, its employees, and its students, the university attorney has an opportunity to practice preventive law.

As an advisor, the university attorney analyzes a situation and advises on its legal ramifications and on the various options being considered for dealing with the situation. In the advisor role, the university attorney can review a proposed policy to ensure that the rights of all parties involved are protected. Counsel can also offer suggestions for additions to the policy.

The particular uses that an institution and its administrators make of the university attorney will be defined by the nature of the institution. At most institutions, a university attorney can and should participate in policy development and implementation as well as in resolution of individual problems. University administrators generally determine the types of policies that are necessary or desirable for the institution. The university attorney can assist these administrators by putting their ideas into a format that clearly advises all parties of the policy and of its applicability to any particular individual. Counsel can also make administrators aware of changes in the law that make new policies necessary.

Student-Related Matters. For the student affairs administrator, effective confrontation of the legal issues related to students is essential. As Chapter
Three indicates, the concept of a contractual relationship between the student
and the institution is receiving increased judicial confirmation. "Courts are
beginning to consider college registration as an implied contractual agreement
between buyer and seller and to interpret the college catalog as a form of institutional advertising" (Marske and Vago, 1980, p. 174). Because many courts
are now viewing university policies and procedures as contractual agreements
(Buss, 1979), university counsel can help to minimize, if not to prevent, legal
problems by being directly involved in the drafting of such policies and procedures. Counsel can also provide assistance in revising these policies as problems arise in individual situations. Counsel can also devise methods for applying the policies in unique situations.

To illustrate, the housing office of a major state university in Illinois
received a request from an incoming freshman to provide him with on-campus
dormitory living arrangements in the school's seventeen-story residential complex. This individual suffered from an extreme allergic reaction both to chicken
and to chicken by-products. At first, the institutional housing administrators
felt that the problems that the situation might create were so enormous that
they should refuse to provide this individual with the housing requested.
When the incoming student and his family insisted that it was his right to be
provided with on-campus living space despite the potential medical risk, the
university housing administrators went to university legal counsel to seek
guidance.

University legal counsel advised the housing administrators that a document could be prepared that, when signed both by the student and by his
legal representative, would minimize, but not eliminate, the potential risk of
liability to the institution. Counsel made it clear that the ultimate decision to
provide housing to the student had to be made by the housing administrators.
If they determined that the risk was too great because the housing complex in
question served more than one million meals per year, the university could
deny on-campus housing to the individual, but that decision had potential
legal risks. Counsel noted that the student could file an action against the university under Section 504 of the Rehabilitation Act of 1973. Counsel noted
also, however, that, should such an action be filed, the standard against which
the institution would be judged was whether it had reasonably attempted to
accommodate the individual's handicap.

In determining whether a reasonable attempt to accommodate the student's handicap had been made, the housing administrators advised counsel
that they had offered to waive the requirement that incoming freshmen must
live in university-approved housing. In addition, they had offered to waive the
same requirement for a high school classmate with whom the student wanted to
room in the housing facility in question. Finally, the housing administrators
offered to locate either a private residence or a smaller private dormitory in
which the two young men could live. University counsel advised the housing

administrators that, in her legal opinion, this was a reasonable accommodation. However, the student rejected the offer.

Next, the housing administrators discussed their options for dealing with the situation and the legal ramifications of each option with legal counsel. Ultimately, the housing administrators decided to allow the student to live in the facility that he had requested. Once they had made that decision, they asked university counsel to prepare a document for the student's signature that would minimize the university's potential risk in having an individual with an extreme allergic condition live in a residence hall facility of that size. University counsel prepared the requested document, which was signed by the student and by his legal representative.

As this example shows, the university attorney did not decide whether the incoming freshman should be allowed to live in the on-campus housing facility. Instead, counsel provided housing administrators with information on the alternatives and on each alternative's legal ramifications that allowed them to exercise their administrative judgment in resolving the issue. Counsel can provide university administrators in all areas with information on the legal effect of proposed decisions and thereby enable them to make informed administrative and managerial decisions. Counsel of this sort is used at least on a daily basis in many major institutions. The process seems work well both for administrators and for university attorneys, and it is the very heart of preventative law.

University attorneys can also make an institution aware of changes in court interpretations of legal requirements that mandate change in university policy. A recent example can be found in the case of *Widmar* v. *Vincent* (1981), in which the United States Supreme Court declared that, once a university opens its premises to use by organized student groups, it cannot discriminate against religious groups on the basis of the content of their speech. At one state university, recognized student organizations are provided, as a privilege of their recognized student organization status, with free space in which to hold organizational meetings. Concurrently, the institution had a policy which prohibited the provision of free meeting space to any organization, including recognized student organizations, if the major purpose of the meeting was to hold a religious service. The *Widmar* decision necessitated a change in institutional policy. After university counsel made the institution aware that its policy needed to change, counsel was instrumental in preparing an amendment to the board of trustees policy that reflected the change in interpretation of the law by the United States Supreme Court. University counsel made it clear, however, that the university could still regulate the time, manner, and place of such meetings, just as it did for other groups.

Another area in which university counsel is involved with student concerns is the area of due process. (See Chapter Two in this volume.) There are two distinct categories of due process: academic due process and disciplinary due process.

The requirements of due process that must be afforded to students in matters of an academic nature are not nearly as stringent as the requirements of due process in matters concerning disciplinary action.

In *Board of Curators of the University of Missouri* v. *Horowitz* (1978), the United States Supreme Court reconfirmed a long-standing tradition of the American court system to stay out of the academic arena. The university had dismissed a medical student, who was close to graduation and who had received excellent grades on her written examinations, for deficiencies in her clinical performance, peer and patient relations, and personal hygiene. Some faculty members had repeatedly expressed dissatisfaction with her work. On evaluation, university counsel recommended that the student not be allowed to graduate on time and that, "absent radical improvement" in the remainder of the year, she be dropped from the program. The student was allowed to take a special set of oral and practical examinations administered by practicing physicians. Although several letters of recommendation were written in her favor, the school decided to drop her from the program. It was this decision that she challenged in court. The Supreme Court affirmed that academic due process does not require an adversarial hearing. All rights of the student in an academic dismissal are met when the institution informs the student of the inadequacies of the student's performance and of their consequences on the student's academic standing. When an institution reviews academic dismissal policies, it is prudent, however, to clear those policies with its attorney.

In contrast to academic due process, disciplinary due process requires far more comprehensive procedural protection for the student. Besides meeting the requirement that the student must know what is expected, allegations of violation of disciplinary standards must advise students of the specific standard violated and allow them to present arguments and testimony on their behalf. In addition, the decision must be made by an impartial fact finder. The impartial fact finder can be a university administrator as long as the administrator has not exhibited bias about the outcome of the proceeding.

The landmark case on the issue of disciplinary due process is *Dixon* v. *Alabama State Board of Education* (1961). *Dixon* centered on the question of whether due process requires a state school to afford students notice and an opportunity for hearing before they are expelled for disciplinary misconduct. Answering in the affirmative, the court provided guidance to public colleges and universities regarding disciplinary procedures by promulgating certain minimum standards, which Ardaiolo discusses in Chapter Two. Legal counsel can help an institution to ensure that its policies and actions afford students all the due process to which they are entitled.

Whenever university policies and procedures are being developed or revised, university counsel should be asked to review the drafts. Legal counsel can help to ensure that policies contain no ambiguities that may create legal disputes with students. Active participation by legal counsel in policy formation is a critical element of preventive law in higher education.

Employee-Related Matters. Unique legal issues are created by employees as well as by students. Although university-employee relationships involve many of the same legal issues as other employer-employee relationships, the university setting involves some special aspects, with which the university attorney should be familiar; these aspects include tenure, term versus continuing contracts, and state civil service systems.

The expanding area of employment law has created another major area of involvement for the university attorney. Student affairs administrators must be aware of the types of employees who work within their area and with the special considerations applicable to each type of employment. Faculty who work within student affairs are generally governed by the policies and procedures that control all academic employees. Any other policies that apply to them as a result of their involvement in student affairs should be pointed out. If the institution has civil service employees or union employees, the administrator must become fauiliar with the terms and conditions unique to such employees. There may be special rules on graduate assistants and student workers. Information of importance in such employment relationships can generally be located in the graduate school and in the office of student work or financial assistance, respectively. Whatever the classification of the employment at issue, it is imperative for each employee to know the chain of command that must be followed. The administrator must make sure that these lines of communication are well in place and known to all. It is also important for each employee to know the appropriate channel or procedure to be used in resolving employment-related problems.

A contractual relationship is generally at the core of any employment relationship, but various statutes and regulations concerning labor and equal employment opportunity (antidiscrimination) are becoming increasingly visible. To complicate the situation, institutions are sometimes faced with competing and conflicting requirements of state and federal regulations. University counsel can help to make the institution aware of the regulations that it must take into consideration in developing its personnel policies and practices. Counsel can also spot potential problems at a time when immediate action can prevent a legal problem that might otherwise result in litigation from developing. Early action can save precious resources for the institution.

The combination of questionable economic stability and heightened awareness among individuals of their rights has resulted in an increasing number of internal grievances and complaints filed with administrative agencies and courts, especially when an institution determines that the services of an individual are no longer required. To make matters worse, colleges and universities traditionally have ignored the concept of long-range planning for reductions in force that various factors can necessitate. As a result, institutions deal with problems as they arise without ever having planned for them. Planning is a major part of preventive law. University counsel, particularly if counsel is a full-time member of the institutional staff, is in an ideal position to help plan for reductions when and if they become necessary.

University counsel has a unique perspective on the institution that few private practitioners can have. Counsel is familiar with the overall organizational structure as well as the institution's goals and objectives. Counsel is also aware of the changes in direction that the institution may be taking in response to competition between needs and resources. This insider's view allows university counsel to work with the institution's administrators to plan for situations that might otherwise have an adverse impact on its overall operation.

To demonstrate, an employee does not always understand the difference between termination of the employee's contractual relationship with the institution and failure to renew the contractual arrangement. The employee knows only that he or she no longer has a job. If the employment outlook is bleak, the employee may seek redress in the administrative or judicial arena. Such a move becomes less likely if the rights of the employee and the institution have been clearly defined. If a person is hired on a term contract, the institution's policies should reflect its right not to renew the contract; policy should also specify the amount of notice to which the employee in entitled if the institution declines to renew the contract.

Termination of employment connotes that the contractual arrangement is obviated during the period of the contract. Generally speaking, termination is legally permissible only where there is just cause for such termination or for reasons clearly specified in the contractual arrangement. The most familiar example, of course, is that of tenured faculty members. A tenured faculty member can generally be terminated only for cause, a condition that has been the subject of great dispute in the courts. Other specified reasons for termination of a tenured faculty member include financial exigency of the institution and program discontinuance.

Early planning provides an institution with the maximum flexibility necessary for operation today. Clear policies also help to prevent unwarranted expectations on the part of employees with respect to continued employment. University counsel can also help to avoid future legal problems by explaining other general elements of the contractual relationship to administrators responsible for the hiring process as well as their obligation to base employment decisions only on employment-related factors.

Most institutional employment contracts are in writing. Generally, they are limited to the terms and conditions specified in writing. However, there are some general exceptions to this rule. When an administrator makes a verbal promise to an employee and when the administrator appears to have the authority to make such a promise, the institution can be bound. For example, where a notice of nonrenewal has been sent to an employee and an administrator tells the employee to ignore the notice, the institution can be bound to the administrator's representation. Such an occurrence creates bad feelings on both sides; in addition, the institution is liable for employment of the individual until timely and effective notice can be given. University counsel can help to prevent such situations by assisting in the training of supervisory personnel. When administrators are aware of the potential hazard that a seemingly innocent remark can pose, they become better able to avoid future legal difficulties.

In addition, university documents that affect the contractual rights of employees should be reviewed. It is a basic rule of contract law that the court will not look to sources outside the contract itself if the terms of the contract are clear and complete. Most institutions have not limited their contractual employment relationship to institutional policies and employment contracts. Several documents can play some role. The best known of such documents is the faculty or employee handbook. Counsel can help to ensure that representations in such documents do not conflict with employment contracts or university policies. Consistency of the terms in a handbook is a prime aspect of preventive law.

Even if none of the situations just described ever arises, legal counsel should be consulted to determine that due process requirements have been met for any employee who is terminated or who is not rehired. As in the case of students, where due process has different requirements for academic matters and disciplinary matters, there are different requirements for the due process owed to employees whose contracts are not renewed and employees whose employment is terminated during the contract period. In *Board of Regents* v. *Roth* (1972), the Supreme Court recognized and described the distinction between dismissal for cause and nonretention: "As a matter of statutory law, a tenured teacher cannot be 'discharged except for cause upon written charges' and pursuant to certain procedures. A nontenured teacher, similarly, is protected to some extent *during* his one-year term. Rules promulgated by the Board of Regents provide that a nontenured teacher dismissed before the end of the year may have some opportunity for review of the 'dismissal.' But, the Rules provide no real protection for a nontenured teacher who simply is not re-employed for the next year" (*Board of Regents* v. *Roth*, 1972, at 567).

When the contractual arrangement is clear and unambiguous, the elements of due process that must be afforded will also be clear and unambiguous. The university counsel can be instrumental in making sure that the language of all relevant documents is clear and unambiguous. Involvement by legal counsel is beneficial in many areas of university administration, not just in student and employee matters.

Governance and Management Issues. A major component of the practice of preventive law requires counsel to sensitize administrators to potential areas of legal risk. As a sophisticated legal consumer, the student affairs administrator can utilize counsel with the specific purpose of identifying potential legal problems. Sensenbrenner (1974, p. 13) identified the high-risk areas in which involvement by university counsel can be most beneficial: "In the student area, university catalogs, application forms, disciplinary procedures, grievance or grade appeal procedures, and student government relationships with the university are . . . problems to be avoided." If athletics falls within the auspices of student affairs, other problem areas of concern to student affairs administrators can include student athletes, financial aid, and eligibility.

As already stated, litigation in any of these areas can be avoided if counsel is aware of the problem as it emerges and if counsel advises on corrective action that can be taken. Involvement by legal counsel will not always prevent legal problems, but it will allow defensive action to be taken before the situation gets out of hand.

Sexual Harassment. One issue in which legal advice can be helpful to universities today is the issue of sexual harassment. In the employment area, sexual harassment is a violation of Title VII of the Civil Rights Act of 1964, as amended. The Equal Employment Opportunity Commission, which has responsibility for enforcement of Title VII, promulgated guidelines that define sexual harassment as "unwelcome sexual advances, requests for sexual favors, and other verbal or physical conduct of a sexual nature . . . constitute sexual harassment when (1) submission to such conduct is made either explicitly or implicitly a term or condition of the individual's employment, (2) submission to or rejection of such conduct by an individual is used as the basis for employment decisions affecting such individual, or (3) such conduct has the purpose or effect of unreasonably interfering with an individual's work performance or creating an intimidating, hostile or offensive working environment" (Code of Federal Regulations, Title 29, Sect. 1604.11, p. 137).

While there are no specific guidelines for students who are not also employees a student can bring a charge of sexual harassment against a professor, the university, or both on the allegation that the student's grade or advancement in a program was adversely affected by the student's refusal to accede to the professor's sexual demands. Although this would not be cause for action under Title VII, it most certainly is cause for action under Title IX of the Educational Amendments of 1972. Title IX prohibits an institution that receives federal financial assistance from discriminating against any recipient of the benefit on the basis of sex.

No matter who the parties are to a charge of sexual harassment, the situation needs to be approached expeditiously, diplomatically, and discretely. The rights of both parties must be protected. It is no more correct to assume that an allegation of sexual harassment is true than it is to assume that an individual charged with a criminal offense is guilty. The problem is the same in both situations. Once an allegation becomes public, the alleged perpetrator of the offense carries the stigma of having committed the act, whether the allegation is valid or not. It is essential for the procedures developed and implemented to deal with situations such as this to protect the rights of all parties. Prompt investigative and corrective action, if necessary, must be the rule. Timely corrective action provides a basis for legal defense if the individual who feels harassed initiates legal action against the institution. The institution can be found liable if it fails to take prompt corrective action.

In the sensitive area of sexual harassment, university counsel can be instrumental in a number of ways. Counsel can help to draft a university policy that states conclusively that sexual harassment will not be condoned either in the employment situation or in the faculty-student situation. Such a policy must exist before the university can take disciplinary action against a violator. In extreme situations, termination of an individual's employment with the institution may be the only solution. When and if such action becomes necessary, the institution must have the authority to terminate the harasser. The source of that authority will be in policy generated by the governing board, which says that such behavior cannot be tolerated and that termination can be imposed when an employee has been found guilty of sexual harassment. Involvement and consultation by legal counsel can be useful at any stage of a proceeding prompted by allegations of sexual harassment.

Copyright Law. Another major concern that has required increased involvement by legal counsel during the last five years originates with changes in copyright law. The first major revision in copyright law since 1909 occurred with passage of the Copyright Act of 1976, which became effective on January 1, 1978. Public institutions of higher education lost the exemption from compliance with copyright law that previously accompanied their status as public entities. Professors can no longer make copies of printed materials to be used for any teaching purpose that they desire. Confusion has emerged, and legal counsel often receives direct inquiries from faculty with regard to copyright questions. To illustrate, a professor wanted to copy a poem and distribute it to his class as part of a sampling of poetic styles. In past years, the professor used the same set of examples each semester. As a result of seminars held on campus to alert faculty and staff to changes in copyright law and of the suggestion that employees should contact university counsel if they had questions, the professor wanted to ensure that he could continue his past practice. The professor explained his usual practice to counsel. To his dismay, legal counsel explained that, while his usual practice was legal under the old copyright law, it would violate the new law. The professor's reply was, "I guess I'll just have to break the law." The professor was assured that his goal could be reached in a lawful manner with the assistance of legal counsel and a little planning. Copying must meet the tests of brevity and spontaneity, it must meet the cumulative effect test, and each copy must include a notice of copyrights ("Agreement in Guidelines. . . , 1976). Counsel explained that the professor could make copies of the poem in question only for use in his current class. In the time remaining before the next semester, the copyright holder of the poem was contacted to request permission to use the poem in the manner described. Permission was obtained without a licensing cost to the professor. Now he uses the poem as he desires, but in a lawful manner.

Contracts. Every university enters into many contracts besides employment and enrollment contracts. Whenever a contract situation is proposed to the university, legal counsel should be consulted. The structure of each institution determines which individuals have the authority to bind the institution lawfully. Legal counsel can assure that authority to sign the particular contract has been properly delegated to the signator. In public institutions, the statutes that create the governing board or the board's charter and bylaws generally empower it with ultimate authority and responsibility for management of the institution. Most private institutions have a corporate charter that delineates the exercise of management responsibility. Whichever instruments are relevant, delegation of certain powers to administrators is necessary for successful operation of the institution. The lines of delegation must be known and carefully observed. An individual who has apparent but not actual authority to bind an institution to a contract may find that he or she is personally liable for performance of the contract.

Even when an individual has actual authority to enter into a contract, there always are terms to which an institution cannot or should not agree. Review by legal counsel of a proposed contract can determine whether proper contracting authority is possessed by the proposed signator and whether the terms of the contract are acceptable to the institution.

Legal Counsel as Advocate

Legal counsel plays an advisory role more often than it plays an adversarial role, but both roles are extremely important to the effective functioning of an institution. The roles are often combined when legal counsel deals with local, state, or federal agencies. The role of legal counsel as advocate is evident once the battle lines have been drawn. For the layman, the general picture raised by legal counsel as advocate is one of an individual in a three-piece pinstriped suit badgering a witness in a courtroom, much like Perry Mason. It is true that that is what an advocate can be.

External Agencies. Given the large number of agencies with which an institution must deal, university counsel can play many roles where an external agency is involved. Sometimes, external agencies, such as the Department of Education, its Office for Civil Rights, the Department of Labor's Office of Federal Contract Compliance Programs, or various other agencies, conduct compliance reviews. Compliance reviews are conducted to ensure that an institution is meeting its state and federal obligations under various statutes. It is possible, however, that the external agency is using the compliance review to gather data that can enable it to determine whether the institution is guilty of violating the rights of an employee or student guaranteed under a statute that the agency enforces. For this reason, university counsel must be involved in preparation of the institution's response, because it can later be used against the institution as an admission of guilt. Involvement by university counsel also provides a mechanism to ensure that the rights to privacy of both students and employees are protected when the data are being provided.

The most visible role played by university counsel in an institution's dealings with external agencies is that of advocate in an adversarial relationship. Whenever a student or employee files a complaint with an external agency, such as a state fair employment practices commission, the Equal Employment Opportunity Commission, the Department of Education, or a court of law, counsel will be greatly aided by close association with the office in which the problem arises. An attorney who is aware of a problem when it first develops can preserve the information necessary to defend the institution in any proceeding that becomes necessary. Legal counsel is also in the best possible position to prepare a legal defense by ensuring that the institution has met all its legal obligations in the situation. All legal problems cannot be avoided, but involvement by a university attorney early in the process, whether in planning or in resolution of individual problems, places the university attorney in the best possible position to manage a situation from the legal perspective. If and when it is required, counsel can act as an interface between university units and external agencies.

However, even if counsel has been involved from an early stage, it is not always possible to prevent a problem or even to convince an individual who feels harmed that he or she has been done no wrong, at least from the legal perspective. There is no way to eliminate the necessity for litigation in a university setting, but early and consistent involvement by university counsel in the overall operation of the institution will minimize the adversity that an institution suffers when an adversarial proceeding has been instituted.

Litigation. No matter how thorough an institution's efforts at prevention are, litigation will occur. When it does, legal counsel must marshall the resources necessary to present the position of the university in the most favorable light possible. In order to do so, counsel must have all relevant information. Student affairs administrators are in a position to make this information available. It is imperative for them to share all information with counsel. Only an attorney has the expertise necessary to determine which information is legally relevant.

All involved parties for the institution should meet with legal counsel to ensure that they understand the nature of the proceeding at issue. Some administrative procedures, like a fact-finding conference with a state human rights agency, are relatively informal. Others, like administrative hearings and court proceedings, require formal rules of evidence to be followed. In all situations, the university must present the facts through its administrators and employees, not through legal counsel.

However, counsel can play an active role when the facts are presented in less formal settings. In all cases, legal counsel should prepare all witnesses thoroughly, so they understand the nature of the proceeding and what is likely to occur. Potential witnesses should not be afraid to ask counsel about anything that they do not understand. Preparation is the key. A witness cannot look to counsel for an answer during the proceeding. It is impossible to plan for each question, but there is no reason to be surprised by the procedure. Legal counsel should advise witnesses always to tell the truth but always to answer only the question actually asked. Potential witnesses should be encouraged not to volunteer information.

A Word of Advice. Every administrator should keep a written record of the efforts or actions taken with respect to a given situation, whether it is one of problem prevention or of early resolution. Where employee or student problems have potential for a grievance or lawsuit, the records that administrators maintain can later become evidence that establishes the university's defense. For example, letters to an employee identifying work-related problems and giving the employee an opportunity to correct them may some day prove that the university was fully within its legal rights to terminate the employee and that the employee received all the due process required under the circumstances. If an administrator determines that informal action is more likely to resolve the problem, notes in a personal file can help the administrator if he or she must testify about the action at a later date. A long time can elapse between the emergence of a problem and its resolution in court. Good record keeping is essential for success.

Conclusion

Legal counsel plays an important role in defense of litigation. However, the primary thrust of an attorney's responsibility to a university and the primary definition of the attorney's role with respect to the institution lies in providing preventive advice that can save the institution from formal litigation or other challenges to its management decisions (Bickel, 1974, p. 73).

A university attorney works with many units of the university on a day-to-day basis. In-house counsel can become familiar with the operations of university units and be available to deal with problems when they arise. Prompt consultation with the university attorney can prevent miscommunication in minor incidents from becoming full-blown conflicts that result in lawsuits. The ability to take prompt and corrective action and to gather information to ensure a defense if litigation cannot be prevented makes the role of university counsel vital to the effective functioning both of student affairs and of other university units.

A word of caution: A university attorney cannot cure all institutional ills. Some administrators may wish to defer to an individual who possesses legal expertise when making administrative decisions. The university attorney is not an administrator. Legal counsel is certainly an essential part of the administrative team, but an attorney is a resource to be used, not abused. The ultimate authority for the management and operation of an institution lies with the administrator appointed by the governing board. The university attorney can help to identify potential legal problems, to determine the positive and negative aspects of actions being considered, and to suggest legally sound alternatives. Even if a university attorney advises that a certain action being considered by a university administrator is legally unsound, it is still the right of that administrator to choose the action that he or she deems most appropriate, despite the legal advice given.

80

References

"Agreement on Guidelines for Classroom Copying In Not-for-Profit Educational Institutions." *Federal Register,* 1976, *45,* 5681–5683.

Bickel, R. D. "The Role of College or University Legal Counsel." *Journal of Law and Education,* 1974, *3,* 73–82.

Buss, W. "Easy Cases Make Bad Law." *Iowa Law Review,* 1979, *65,* 1–15.

Marske, C., and Vago, S. "Law and Disputed Processing in the Academic Community." *Judicature,* 1980, *64,* 165–178.

Sensenbrenner, R. "University Counsel: Law, Logic, and Logistics." *Journal of College and University Law,* 1974, *2,* 13–18.

Shari Rhode is chief trial attorney at Southern Illinois University Carbondale, where she has been employed in the Office of University Legal Counsel since 1976. A member of the Illinois Bar Association, the American Bar Association, the Federal Bar Association, the National Association of College and University Attorneys, and the Defense Research Institute, she has participated in presentations to the American Council on Education, the Illinois State Bar Association, and the State Universities Civil Service System.

Specific sources of additional information including periodicals and hot lines are discussed.

Conclusion and Sources of Additional Assistance

Margaret J. Barr

Student affairs administration can be a difficult task. Depending on the size, complexity, and mission of the particular student affairs unit, a number of activities, services, and programs have legal implications. In this volume, the authors attempt to provide a framework for understanding the many sources of legal constraints that influence both policy and action. Certainly, all topics of concern to the student affairs administrator have not been covered. Instead, the emphasis has been placed on providing an overview of common issues and on highlighting emerging areas of concern. In each chapter, advice was given that practitioners can use in their day-to-day activities.

Every author stressed that student affairs administrators must understand the unique legal status of their institution and how that status can influence administrative practice. Every author stressed the need for informal legal advice as a preventive measure that could avoid litigation and legal complexities. In Chapter Two, Ardaiolo underlines the importance of a doctrine of fundamental fairness and reasonableness in dealing with student discipline situations. As Shur points out in Chapter Three, the growing body of case law that defines the student-institution relationship as contractual in nature highlights the need for organized review of institutional policies and publications. Shur suggests standards that can serve as useful reminders to us all as we deal with these complex issues. In Chapter Five, Cuyjet, Gilbert, and Conboy

M. J. Barr (Ed.). *Student Affairs and the Law.* New Directions for
Student Services, no. 22. San Francisco: Jossey-Bass, June 1983.

stress the need for precision, both in development and in implementation of policy concerning student organizations.

Facility use policies are also becoming important to sound management. Student affairs administrators cannot rely on past practice but must have sound policy guidelines to guide decision. As Barr notes in Chapter Four, facility use has received relatively little judicial attention to date, but it seems to be an area in which activity will increase in the future. Here as elsewhere, prevention is the key.

Finally, the student affairs administrator with legal concerns has an effective partner in legal counsel. Rhode argues in Chapter Six that early involvement of legal counsel can reduce potential problems, help to solve issues within a legal framework, and prepare for litigation if legal action is necessary.

Knowledge, precision, written documentation, periodic policy review, and sound legal advice are central to effective management in a complex and ever changing legal environment. This volume is a first step for the administrator who wishes to have basic knowledge of the interaction between student affairs and the law. The list of sources of additional assistance that follows will help the reader to expand that base.

Books

Alexander, K., and Solomon, E. *College and University Law.* Charlottesville, Va.: Michie, 1972.

This volume provides a broad-based understanding of the relationship between education and the law. Although it is dated and it was not written specifically for the lay person, it will help the reader to understand the broad legal issues that influence higher education.

Kaplin, W. A. *The Law of Higher Education: Legal Implications of Administrative Decision Making.* San Francisco: Jossey-Bass, 1978.

This book, written in easily understood language, covers the entire postsecondary spectrum. Of particular value to the student affairs administrator are the sections on personal liability, the college and the student, and the college and the federal government.

Hollander, P. A. *A Legal Handbook for Educators.* Boulder, Colo.: Westview Press, 1978.

Although it is not as broad-based as the two works just cited, this volume has merit. It is written in lay language and organized in a clear and concise manner.

Periodical Sources

Journal of College and University Law, a quarterly publication of the National Association of College and University Attorneys, is addressed to lawyers, but the style is appropriate to the lay person, and the issues covered often have implications for student affairs administrators.

Young, D. P., and Gehring, D. D. (Eds.). *The College Student and the Courts.* Asheville, N.C.: College Administration Publications, 1973.

This volume is updated quarterly by the addition of new pertinent cases. A review is provided for each case, and supporting commentary is given. The focus is on students, so the volume is particularly useful to the student affairs administrator.

The Chronicle of Higher Education is published 48 times a year by the Chronicle of Higher Education, Inc., 1333 New Hampshire Avenue, Washington, D.C., and provides substantial coverage of legal and statutory developments.

Higher Education and National Affairs, a weekly publication of the American Council on Education, provides in-depth coverage of applicable statutory and regulatory sections emanating from Washington.

Business Officer, a monthly publication of the National Association of College and University Business Officers, is available only to members. It can be very useful to the practicing administrator, particularly in the area of regulatory change.

Hotlines

Three updated telephone hotlines provide information on the status of current legislation:

Higher Education—(800) 424-2973 after 5 P.M. Eastern Standard Time

National Association of Student Financial Aid Administrators
   (202) 785-0451 (twenty-four hours)

National Association of State Universities and Land Grant Colleges
   (202) 293-4293 (twenty-four hours)

Margaret J. Barr is vice-president for student affairs at Northern Illinois University, DeKalb.

Appendixes

APPENDIX 1.

Glossary of Legal Terms

Appeal: Resort to a superior court for review of a decision by an inferior court. On the state level, most appeals are taken from the trial level to an intermediate court and then to the highest court in the state. On the federal level, appeals are taken from the federal district court to the appropriate circuit court of appeals, then to the United States Supreme Court. In some instances on both the state and federal levels, appeals can be taken directly to the highest court.

Certiorari, writ of: The Latin term means *to be informed of.* In the United States, the writ of certiorari is used by the United States Supreme Court as a discretionary device to choose the cases that it wishes to hear. If the writ is denied, the Supreme Court declines to hear the case, and the decision of the lower court becomes final. If the writ is accepted, the lower court must turn all relevant documents over to the Supreme Court. The trend in state courts has been to abolish the writ. *Certiorari* is sometimes abbreviated, as in the expression *cert. denied.* The meaning is the same.

Civil: In legal terminology, *civil* contrasts with *criminal.* A civil action is instituted by a private individual seeking redress, usually monetary, for a harm done by another.

Common law: That body of law, dating back to antiquity, brought to the United States from England. The term *common law* is often used in contrast with the term *statutory law*, meaning laws enacted by legislative action.

Criminal: In legal terminology, *criminal* constrasts with *civil.* In a criminal action, the state brings an action against the wrongdoer on behalf of the person harmed. Since the law that was broken was made by the state legislature, is is actually the state that was wronged. A person found guilty of a criminal offense can be incarcerated, fined, or both.

Decree: A declaration of the court announcing the legal consequences of the facts found.

Demurrer: An admission by a defendant that the allegations set out in the complaint against him are true, but they are not sufficient to form a cause of action against him.

Deposition: The testimony of a witness under oath, taken outside of court, usually in the office of a lawyer. A word-by-word account of the deposition is taken in writing, and this transcript is admissible in court. Depositions are useful for taking the testimony of witnesses immediately after the disputed occurrence, while the memory is still fresh. Depositions are used as part of pretrial discovery.

Discovery: Pretrial devices used by one party to obtain facts and information about the case from the other party. This information is used in preparing the case for trial. The trend in the United States is toward liberal use of discovery devices. Discovery enables opposing lawyers to find out all there is to know about the case before they get to trial. In many instances, discovery results in out-of-court settlements, because the lawyers are able to determine the probable court finding.

Immunity: Exemption from doing something that the law requires. Immunity from prosecution is sometimes granted in exchange for information from a witness, who otherwise would be testifying against himself.

Infra: A Latin word meaning *below, after, later.* In a sentence, it means that the proposition stated in the sentence will appear again or be explained more fully later in the text.

Injunction: A form of relief granted by a court, which forbids a defendant from continuing a certain act or from beginning a certain act.

In re: A Latin term meaning in the matter of, concerning. Found in case names where there are not adverse parties but rather a thing, such as an estate, that is in dispute. For example, *In re: Estate of Smith.*

Interrogatories: A pretrial discovery device consisting of a series of written questions submitted by one party to the other party or to a witness. The person who answers the interrogatories signs a statement swearing that the information given is true.

Liability: In legal terminology, *liability* has a very broad definition. Generally, it means responsibility for possible or actual loss, penalty, evil, expense, or burden. *Liability* is often used to mean *liability for damages,* an amount determined by a trial of the facts of the case.

Malice: Intent, without just cause or reason, to commit an unlawful act that will result in injury to another or others.

Mandamus, writ of: The Latin word means *we command.* An order by a superior court to an inferior court commanding it to perform the act specified in the writ. A writ of mandamus is an extraordinary remedy, used only in drastic situations. Writs of mandamus can also be issued to corporations and their officers, executive and judicial officers, and other public officials, commanding them to perform an act within the scope of their particular authority.

Remand: To send a case from the superior court back to the court from which it came for the purpose of having some further action taken.

Respondeat superior: A Latin term meaning let the master answer. The legal doctrine that holds a master responsible for the wrongful acts of his servant if the acts are committed while the servant is engaged in his master's business. This doctrine holds for a principal-agent relationship.

Statutory law: The body of law created by legislative enactments. Statutory law is often contrasted with common law.

Supra: A Latin word meaning *above* or *over.* In a sentence, *supra* indicates that the proposition stated in the sentence was stated earlier in the text.

Tort: A violation of a duty that results in a private or civil wrong or injury for which a court can provide a remedy in the form of an action for damages.

An intentional tort is a wrong done by one who intends to perform an act that the law forbids. Compare this with negligence. In negligence, the tortfeasor — that is, the one who commits the tort — has failed to exercise the requisite standard of care in performing an otherwise permissible act.

APPENDIX 2.

List of Cases

Aman v. *Handler*, 653 F.2d 41 (1st Cir. 1981).

American Civil Liberties Union of Southern California v. *Board of Education, City of Los Angeles*, 55 Cal. 2d 906, 359 P.2d 57 (1961).

American Civil Liberties Union of Southern California v. *Board of Education, City of San Diego*, 55 Cal. 2d 167, 359 P.2d 45 (1961).

American Civil Liberties Union of Virginia v. *Radford College*, 315 F. Supp. 893 (W.D. Va. 1970).

American Futures Systems, Inc. v. *Pennsylvania State University*, 464 F. Supp. 1252 (M.D. Pa. 1979); 618 F.2d 252 (ed. Cir. 1980); revs'd and remanded (3d. Cir. No. 81-2674, 1982).

Anderson v. *Banks*, 520 F. Supp. 472 (S.D. Ga. 1981).

Arizona Board of Regents v. *Harper*, 108 Ariz. 223, 495 P.2d 453 (1972).

Associated Students, Etc. v. *Trustees of California State Universities and Colleges*, 128 Cal. Rptr. 601, 56 Cal. App. 3d 667 (1st District 1976).

Baldwin v. *Zoradi*, 176 Cal. Rptr, 809, 123 Cal. App. 3d 275 (5th Dist. 1981).

Basch v. *George Washington University*, 370 A.2d 1364 (D.C. Cir. 1977).

Behrand v. *State*, 55 Ohio App. 2d 135, 379 N.E.2d 617 (1977).

Bishop v. *Wood*, 426 U.S. 341, 96 S.Ct. 2074 (1976).

Board of Curators of the University of Missouri v. *Horowitz*, 435 U.S. 78, 90 S.Ct. 948 (1978).

Board of Regents v. *Roth*, 408 U.S. 564 (1972).

Board of Trustees v. *City of Los Angeles*, 122 Cal. Rptr. 361, 49 Cal. App. 3d 45 (2d Dist. 1975).

Brandenberg v. *Ohio*, 393 U. S. 948 (1969).

Bradshaw v. *Rawlings*, 464 F. Supp. 175 (E.D. Pa. 1979), 612 F.2d 135 (3d Cir. 1979).

Brooks v. *Auburn University*, 296 F. Supp. 188 (M.D. Ala. 1969); aff'd 412 F.2d 1171 (5th Cir. 1975).

Brown v. *Oakland*, 51 Cal. App. 2d 150, 124 P.2d 369 (1942).

Buck v. *Carter*, 308 F. Supp. 1246 (W.D. Wis. 1970).

Cafeteria and Restaurant Workers v. *McElroy*, 367 U.S. 886, 895 (1961).

Carroll v. *Kittle*, 203 Kan. 841, 457 P.2d 21 (1969).

Cary v. *Piphus*, 435 U.S. 247, 98 S.Ct. 1042 (1978).

Cazenovia College v. *Patterson*, 45 A.D.2d 501, 360 N.Y.S.2d 94 (1974).

Central Hudson Gas and Elecrtric Corp. v. *Public Service Commission*, 447 U.S. 557 (1980).

Channing Club v. *Board of Regents of Texas Tech University*, 317 F. Supp. 688 (N.D. Tex. 1970).

Chappel v. *Franklin Pierce School District No. 402*, 71 Wash. 2d 17, 426 P.2d 471 (1967).

Chess v. *Widmar*, 480 F. Supp. 907 (W.D. Mo. 1979), 635 F.2d 131 (8th Cir. 1980); *Widmar* v. *Vincent*, 102 S.Ct. 269 (1981).

Cholmakjian v. *Board of Trustees, Michigan State University*, 315 F. Supp. 1335 (W.D. Mich. 1970).

City of Boulder v. *Regents University of Colorado*, 179 Colo. 420, 501 P.2d 123 (1972).

Civil Service Employees Association, Inc. v. *State University of New York at Stony Brook*, 82 Misc.2d 334, 368 N. Y. S.2d 279 (1974).

Connelly v. *University of Vermont*, 244 F. Supp. 156 (D. Vt. 1965).

Cort v. *Ash*, 422 U.S. 66, 95 S.Ct. 2080 (1975).

Craft v. *Board of Trustees of the University of Illinois*, 516 F. Supp. 1317 (N.D. Ill. 1981).

Dixon v. *Alabama State Board of Education*, 294 F.2d 150 (5th Cir. 1961).

Donnelly v. *Suffolk University*, 3 Mass. Ap. Ct. 788, 337 N.E.2d 920 (1976).

Dudley v. *William Penn College*, 219 N.W.2d 484 (Iowa 1974).

Due v. *Florida A. & M. University*, 233 F. Supp. 396 (N.D. Fla. 1963).

Dunkel v. *Elkins*, 325 F. Supp. 1235 (D. Md. 1971).

East Meadows Community Concerts Association v. *Board of Education*, 18 N.Y.2d 129, 219 N.E.2d 172 (1966).

Eisele v. *Ayers*, 63 Ill. App. 3d 1039, 381 N.E.2d 21 (1978).

Esteban v. *Central Missouri State College*, 415 F.2d 1077 (8th Cir. 1969).

Fowler v. *Rhode Island*, 345 U.S. 67, 73 S.Ct. 526 (1953).

French v. *Bashful*, 303 F. Supp. 1333 (E.D. La. 1969).

Furutani v. *Ewigleben*, 297 F. Supp. 1163 (N.D. Cal. 1969).

Gabrilowitz v. *Newman*, 582 F. 2d 100 (1st Cir. 1978).

Gardenshire v. *Chalmers*, 326 F. Supp. 1200 (D. Kansas 1971).

Gaspar v. *Bruton*, 512 F.2d 843 (10th Cir. 1975).

Gay Activists Alliance v. *Board of Regents*, 638 P.2d 1116 (Okla. 1981).

Gay Alliance of Students v. *Matthews*, 544 F.2d 162 (4th Cir. 1976).

Gay Lib v. *University of Missouri*, 58 F.2d 848 (8th Cir. 1977).

Gay Rights v. *Austin Peay State University*, 477 F. Supp. 1267 (M.D. Tenn. 1979).

Gay Students Organization v. *Bonner*, 509 F.2d 652 (1st Cir. 1974).

General Order of Judicial Standards of Procedures and Substance in Review of Student Discipline in Tax-Supported Institutions of Education, 45 F.R.D. 133 (W.D. Mo. 1968).

Giles v. *Howard University*, 428 F. Supp. 603 (D.C. Cir. 1977).

Goldberg v. *Virginia State Bar*, 421 U.S. 773, 95 S.Ct. 2004 (1975).

Greenhill v. *Bailey*, 378 F. Supp. 632 (S.D. Iowa 1975).

Healy v. *James*, 408 U.S. 169, 92 S.Ct. 2338 (1972).

Healy v. *Larsson*, 67 Misc.2d 374, 323 N.Y.S.2d 625 (1971).

Hermann v. *Hiersteiner*, D.C. of Shawnee Co., Docket No. 78CV0612, Division, 1 (1978).

Hines v. *Baker*, 667 F.2d 699 (8th Cir. 1981).

Hunt v. *McNair*, 413 U.S. 734, 93 S.Ct. 2868 (1973).

Ianiello v. *University of Bridgeport*, Conn. Trial Ct. (1977).

International Society for Krishna Consciousness of Atlanta et al. v. *Eaves*, 601 F.2d 809 (5th Cir. 1979).

Jones v. *Board of Regents of University of Arizona*, 436 F.2d 618 (9th Cir. 1970).

Jones v. *Vassar College*, 59 Misc.2d 296, 299 N.Y.S.2d 283 (1969).

Keegan v. *University of Delaware*, 349 A.2d 14 (Del. 1975).

Kellam v. *School Board of Norfolk*, 202 Va. 252, 117 S.E.2d 96 (1960).

Keys v. *Sawyer*, 353 F. Supp. 936 (S.D. Tex. 1973).

Krasnow v. *Virginia Polytechnic Institute and State University*, 414 F. Supp. 55 (W.D. Va. 1976).

Lai v. *Board of Trustees of East Carolina University*, 330 F. Supp. 904 (E.D. N.C. 1971).

Lau v. *Nichols*, 414 U.S. 563, 94 S.Ct. 786 (1974).

Lavash v. *Kountze*, 473 F. Supp. 868 (D. Mass. 1979).

Leahy v. *State*, 46 N.Y.S.2d 310 (Ct. of Claims 1944).

Lemon v. *Kurtzman*, 403 U.S. 602, 91 S.Ct. 2105 (1971).

Lieberman v. *Marshall*, 236 So.2d 120 (Fla. 1970).

Lowenthal v. *Vanderbilt University*, Davidson Co., Tennessee, Docket No. A-8325; Memorandum Opinion (1977).

Lowery v. *Adams*, 344 F. Supp. 446 (W.D. Kentucky, 1972).

Lyons v. *Salve Regina College*, 565 F.2d 200 (1st Cir. 1977).

McDonald v. *Hogness*, 598 P.2d 707 (Wash. 1979).

Mahavongsanan v. *Hall*, 529 F.2d 448 (5th Cir. 1969).

Marsh v. *Alabama*, 326 U.S. 501, 66 S.Ct. 276 (1946).

Maryland Public Interest Research Group v. *Elkins*, 565 F.2d 864 (4th Cir. 1977).

Morris v. *Nowotny*, 323 S.W.2d 301 (Tex. Civ. App. 1959); cert. den. 361 U.S. 889, 80 S.Ct. 164 (1959).

Mortiboys v. *St. Michaels College*, 478 F.2d 196 (2d Cir. 1973).

Mozart v. *State*, 109 Misc. 2d 1092, 441 N.Y.S.2d 600 (1981).

National Socialist White Peoples Party v. *Ringers*, 473 F.2d 1010 (4th Cir. 1973).

National Strike Information Center v. *Brandeis University*, 315 F. Supp. 928 (D. Mass. 1970).

New Left Education Project v. *Board of Regents of the University of Texas System*, 326 F. Supp. 158 (W.D. Tex. 1970); 404 U.S. 541, 92 S.Ct. 652 (1972); 414 U.S. 87, 94 S.Ct. 118 (1973).

New Times, Inc. v. *Arizona Board of Regents*, 110 Ariz. 367, 519 P.2d 169 (1974).

Niedermeyer v. *Curators of University of Missouri*, 1895.

Owen v. *City of Independence, Missouri*, 445 U.S. 662, 100 S.Ct. 1398 (1980).

Paine v. *Board of Regents of University of Texas System*, 335 F. Supp. 199 (W.D. Texas 1972).

Parker v. *Brown*, 316 U.S. 656, 62 S.Ct. 1266 (1943).

Paynter v. *New York University*, 66 Misc.2d 92, 319 N.Y.S.2d 893 (1971).

Peretti v. *State of Montana*, 464 F. Supp. 784 (D. Mont. 1979); rev'd 661 F.2d 756 (9th Cir. 1981).

Pratt v. *Arizona Board of Regents*, 110 Ariz. 466, 520 P.2d 514 (1974).

Reed v. *Reed*, 404 U.S 71, 92 S. Ct. 251 (1971).

Robertson v. *Haaland*, Penobscot Co. Super. Ct., Docket No. 77-170, slip opinion p. 3 (1977).

Rubtchinsky v. *State University of New York*, 46 Misc.2d 679, 260 N.Y.S.2d 256 (Ct. of Claims 1965).

Saenz v. *University Interscholastic League*, 487 F.2d 1026 (5th Cir. 1976).

Sandoval v. *Board of Regents*, 75 N.M. 261, 403 P.2d 699 (1965).

Sawaya v. *Tucson High School District*, 78 Ariz. 389, 281 P. 2d 105 (1955).

Scheur v. *Rhodes*, 416 U.S. 232, 94 S.Ct. 1683 (1974).

Schuyler v. *State University of New York at Albany*, 31 A.D.2d 273, 297 N.Y.S.2d 368 (1968).

Scott v. *Alabama State Board of Education*, 300 F. Supp. 163 (M.D. Alabama 1969).

Scully v. *State*, 305 N.Y. 707, 112 N.E.2d 782 (1953).

Shamloo v. *Mississippi State Board of Trustees, Etc.*, 620 F.2d 516 (5th Cir. 1980).

Shelton v. *Tucker*, 384 U.S. 479, 81 S.Ct. 247 (1960).

Sill v. *Penn State University*, 318 F. Supp. 608 (M.D. Pa. 1970).

Slaughter v. *Brigham Young University*, 514 F.2d 622 (10th Cir. 1974); cert. den. 423 U.S. 898 (1975).

Smith v. *Ellington*, 334 F. Supp. 90 (E.D. Tenn. 1971).

Soglin v. *Kauffman*, 418 F.2d 163 (7th Cir. 1969).

Spartacus Youth League v. *Board of Trustees of Illinois Industrial University*, 502 F. Supp. 278 (1980).

Splawn v. *Woodard*, 287 S.W. 677 (Tex. Civ. App. 1926).

Stacey v. *Williams*, 306 F. Supp. 963 (N.D. Mis. 1969).

State ex rel. *Curators of the University of Missouri* v. *Neill*, 397 S.W.2d 666 (No. 1966).

State v. *Jordan*, 53 Hawaii 634, 500 P.2d 56 (1972).

Steinberg v. *Chicago Medical School*, 69 Ill. 2d 320, 371 N.E.2d 634 (1977).

Stricklin v. *Regents of University of Wisconsin*, 297 F. Supp. 416 (W.D. Wis. 1969).

Sword v. *Fox*, 446 F.2d 1091 (4th Cir. 1971).

Taylor v. *Wake Forest University*, 16 N.C. App. 117, 191 S.E.2d 379 (1972).

Tedeschi v. *Wagner College*, 49 N.Y.2d 652, 404 N.E.2d 1302 (1980).

Tinker v. *Des Moines Independent School District*, 393 U.S. 503, 89 S.Ct. 733 (1969).

Trustees of Columbia University v. *Jacobsen*, 53 N.J. Super. 574, 148 A.2d 63 (1959).

Turkovich v. *Board of Trustees University of Illinois*, 11 Ill. 2d 460, 143 N.E. 2d 229 (1957).

University of Missouri at Columbia NEA v. *Dalton*, 456 F. Supp. 985 (W.D. Mo. 1978).

University of North Carolina v. *Town of Carrboro*, 15 N.C. App. 501, 190 S.E.2d 231 (1972).

Uzzell v. *Friday*, 625 F.2d 1117 (4th Cir. 1980).

Villyard et al. v. *Regents of University System of Georgia*, 204 Ga. 517, 50 S.E.2d 313 (1948).

Watson v. *Board of Regents of the University of Colorado*, 182 Colo. 307, 512 P.2d 1162 (1973).

Widmar v. *Vincent*, 102 S.Ct. 269 (1981).

Winnick v. *Manning*, 460 F.2d 545 (2d Cir. 1972).

Wood v. *Strickland*, 420 U.S. 308, 95 S.Ct. 992 (1975).

Woodruff v. *West Virginia Board of Regents*, 328 F. Supp. 1023 (D.W. Va. 1971).

Zumbrun v. *University of Southern California*, 101 Cal. Rptr. 449, 25 Cal. App. 3d 1 (1972).

Index

A

Academic sanctions: and contractual relationships, 29–31; and student discipline, 16, 17–18, 23–24

Admissions, and contractual relationships, 29

Aiken, R. J., 18, 11, 46, 52

Alabama: *Dixon* case in, 15–16, 35, 71, 92; due process in, 20, 94; facility use in, 41, 43, 91, 93

Alexander, K., 5, 6, 9, 10, 11, 13, 15, 24, 82

Aman v. *Handler,* and student organizations, 57, 91

American Civil Liberties Union of Southern California v. *Board of Education, City of Los Angeles,* and facility use, 44, 91

American Civil Liberties Union of Southern California v. *Board of Education, San Diego,* and facility use, 44, 91

American Civil Liberties Union of Virginia v. *Pennsylvania State University,* and facility use, 43–44, 91

Anderson v. *Banks,* and contractual relationships, 31, 91

Annotated 5, 43, 52

Antitrust laws, and liability, 48–49

Appeal, defined, 87

Arbitrariness, defined, 19

Ardaiolo, F. P., 1, 13–25, 71, 81

Arizona: facility use in, 41, 42, 43, 46, 47, 91, 93, 94; institutional autonomy in, 5

Arizona, University of, and facility use case, 43, 93

Arizona Board of Regents v. *Harper,* and facility use, 46, 91

Associated Students, Etc. v. *Trustees of California State Universities and Colleges,* and student organizations, 59, 91

Association, freedom of, and student organizations, 55

Athletes, contractual relationships with, 36–37

B

Auburn University, and facility use case, 43, 91

Austin Peay State University, and student organization case, 56, 57, 92

Baldwin v. *Zoradi,* and student organizations, 62–63, 91

Bargerstock, C. T., 21, 25

Barr, M. J., 1–12, 39–52, 65, 81–83

Basch v. *George Washington University,* and contractual relationships, 34, 91

Behrand v. *State,* and contractual relationships, 32, 91

Bender, L. W., 28, 38

Bernard, J. L., 21, 24

Bernard, M. L., 21, 24

Bickel, R. D., 79, 80

Bishop v. *Wood,* and contractual relationships, 35, 91

Board of Curators of the University of Missouri v. *Horowitz,* 91; and contractual relationships, 30; and counsel as adviser, 71; and due process, 17–18, 19

Board of Regents v. *Roth,* and counsel as adviser, 74, 91

Board of Trustees v. *City of Los Angeles,* and facility use, 49, 91

Board, governing. *See* Governing boards

Boulder, facility use in, 49, 92

Brandenberg v. *Ohio,* and student organizations, 58, 91

Bradshaw v. *Rawlings,* and student organizations, 61–62, 63, 91

Brandeis University, and student organization case, 59, 93

Bridgeport, University of, and contractual relationship case, 32, 93

Brigham Young University, and contractual relationship case, 35, 94

Brooks v. *Auburn University,* and facility use, 43, 91

Brown v. *Oakland,* and facility use, 47, 91

Brubacher, J. S., 18, 25

46–47; for negligence, 47–48, 60–63; and unfair competition, 49

Lieberman v. *Marshall,* and facility use, 46, 58, 93

Local governments, and liability, 49–50

Local ordinances, authority of, 10

Los Angeles, facility use in, 44, 49, 91

Louisiana, due process in, 22, 92

Lowenthal v. *Vanderbilt University,* and contractual relationships, 32–33, 93

Lowery v. *Adams,* and due process, 20, 93

Lyons v. *Salve Regina College,* and contractual relationships, 31, 93

M

McDonald v. *Hogness,* and contractual relationships, 30, 93

Mahavongsanan v. *Hall,* and contractual relationships, 31, 93

Maine, contractual relationships in, 30, 36

Maine, University of, housing contract at, 36

Malice, defined, 88

Mancuso, J. H., 16, 25

Mandamus, writ of, defined, 88

Marsh v. *Alabama,* and facility use, 41, 93

Marske, C.. 67, 69, 80

Maryland: facility use in, 45, 92; student organizations in, 59, 93

Maryland, University of: and facility use case, 45; and student organization case, 59

Maryland Public Interest Research Group v. *Elkins,* and student organizations, 59, 93

Mass, M. A., 17, 25

Massachusetts: contractual relationships in, 29, 92; student organizations in, 59, 93

Meadows, R. B., 18, 25

Meyers, J. H., 10, 12

Michigan: facility use in, 43, 92; institutional autonomy in, 5

Michigan State University, and facility use case, 43, 92

Minnesota, institutional autonomy in, 5

Mississippi, due process in, 20, 94

Missouri: contractual relationships in, 27, 31, 34, 93; due process in, 16, 46, 92; facility use in, 45, 46, 48, 93, 94; *Horowitz* case in, 17–18, 19, 30, 71, 91;

student organizations in, 54, 57, 92

Missouri, University of: and contractual relationship case, 27, 31, 34, 93; and facility use case, 46, 94; and *Horowitz* case, 17–18, 19, 30, 71, 91; and student organization case, 57, 92

Missouri at Columbia, University of, and facility use case, 45, 94

Missouri at Kansas City, University of, and student organization case, 54

Montana, contractual relationships in, 32, 93

Moos, M., 9, 12

Morrill Act of 1862, 8

Morris v. *Nowotny,* and facility use, 46, 93

Mortiboys v. *St. Michaels College,* and facility use, 47, 93

Mozart v. *State,* and student organization, 55, 61, 63, 93

N

National Association of State Universities and Land Grant Colleges, 83

National Association of Student Financial Aid Administrators, 83

National Socialist White People's Party v. *Ringers,* and facility use, 45, 93

National Strike Information Center v. *Brandeis University,* and student organizations, 59, 93

Negligence, liability for, 47–48, 60–63

Nevada, institutional autonomy in, 5

New Hampshire, student organizations in, 57, 58

New Hampshire, University of, and student organization case, 57, 58

New Left Education Project v. *Board of Regents of the University of Texas System,* and facility use, 42, 93

New Mexico, facility use in, 47, 94

New Times, Inc. v. *Arizona Board of Regents,* and facility use, 42, 93

New York: contractual relationships in, 28, 33, 34, 35, 36, 37, 91, 93, 94; facility use in, 45, 46, 47, 92, 94; student organizations in, 55, 60–61, 63, 93

New York University, and contractual relationship case, 34, 93

Niedermeyer v. *Curators of University of Missouri,* and contractual relationships, 27, 31, 34, 93

Thompson, J., 10. 12
Tice, T. N., 19, 25
Tichbourne, J., 27
Tinker v. *Des Moines Independent School District,* 94; and due process, 15; and facility use, 42; and legal constraints, 4; and student organizations, 55
Title VI, of Civil Rights Act, 8, 48
Title VII, of Civil Rights Act, 75
Title IX, of Educational Amendments, 8, 37, 48, 75
Tort: defined, 88-89; and legal constraints, 8
Trustees. *See* Governing boards
Trustees of Columbia University v. *Jacobsen,* and contractual relationships, 28, 94
Tucson, facility use in, 47, 94
Turkovich v. *Board of Trustees University of Illinois,* and facility use, 46, 94

U

Unification Church, 57
U.S. Court of Appeals: and contractual relationships, 30; and due process, 17; role of, 6; and student organizations, 62
U.S. Supreme Court: and contractual relationships, 30; and due process, 13, 17-18, 19, 23; and facility use, 40, 48; and legal constraints, 4, 6-7; and legal counsel, 70, 71, 74; and student organizations, 54, 55-56, 63-64
University of Missouri at Columbia NEA v. *Dalton,* and facility use, 45, 94
University of North Carolina v. *Town of Carrboro,* and facility use, 49, 94
Utah, contractual relationships in, 35, 94
Uzzell v. *Friday,* and due process, 20, 94

V

Vago, S., 67, 69, 80
Van Alystene, W. A., 3, 12
Vanderbilt University, and contractual relationship case, 32-33, 93
Vassar College, and contractual relationship case, 36, 93
Vermont: contractual relationships in, 30; due process in, 16, 92; facility use in, 47, 93

Vermont, University of, court case involving, 16, 30, 92
Villyard et al. v. *Regents of University System of Georgia,* and facility use, 49, 95
Virginia: due process in, 21, 93; facility use in, 43, 47, 48, 91, 92
Virginia Polytechnic Institute and State University, and due process case, 21, 93

W

Wagner College, and contractual relationship case, 35, 94
Wake Forest University, and contractual relationship case, 37, 94
Washington: contractual relationships in, 30, 93; student organizations in, 62, 91
Washington, University of, School of Medicine of, and contractual relationships, 30
Watson v. *Board of Regents of the University of Colorado,* and facility use, 45, 95
Weisinger, R., 22, 25
West Virginia, due process in, 21, 95
Widmar v. *Vincent,* 92, 95; and counsel as adviser, 70; and student organizations, 54
Wieruszowski, H., 14, 25
William Penn College, and facility use case, 47, 92
Winnick v. *Manning,* and due process, 20, 95
Wisconsin, due process in, 21, 91, 94
Wisconsin, University of, and due process case, 21, 94
Wood v. *Strickland,* 95; and facility use, 48; and student organizations, 63-64
Woodruff v. *West Virginia Board of Regents,* and due process, 21, 95
Wright, C. A., 3, 12

Y

Young, D. P., 7, 12, 15, 19, 25, 83

Z

Zirkel, P. A., 21, 25
Zumbrun v. *University of Southern California,* and contractual relationships, 34, 95